HIDDEN
LEICESTERSHIRE
& RUTLAND

Jeffery W. Whitelaw

COUNTRYSIDE BOOKS
NEWBURY • BERKSHIRE

C000016581

COUNTRYSIDE BOOKS
3 Catherine Road
Newbury, Berkshire

ISBN 1 85306 422 X

Illustrations by Trevor Yorke
from photographs taken by the author.

The front cover photograph shows Bradgate Park
and the back cover shows the Watch Tower, Lyddington,
both taken by the author.

Produced through MRM Associates Ltd., Reading
Typeset by Acorn Bookwork, Salisbury
Printed by J. W. Arrowsmith Ltd., Bristol

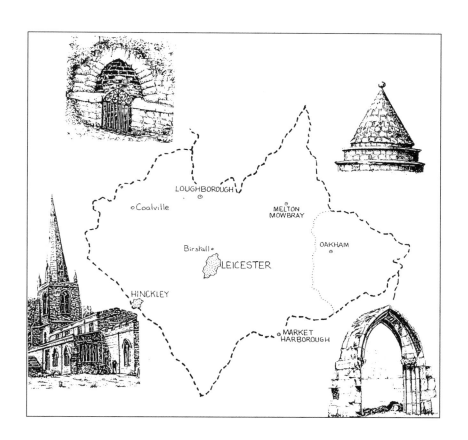

LOUGHBOROUGH

Coalville

MELTON
MOWBRAY

Birstall

OAKHAM

LEICESTER

HINCKLEY

MARKET
HARBOROUGH

INTRODUCTION

—— When I was commissioned to write my previous book in this series, *Hidden Hertfordshire*, I anticipated that, given my 34 years' residence in the county, it would prove to be a proverbial 'piece of cake'. I was wrong – despite the large amount of information I had squirrelled away over those years, I found there was no real substitute for a 'site visit'. With almost double the number of villages in this book than in my previous volume, *Leicestershire and Rutland* was a yet more daunting prospect and I covered nearly 3,000 miles in the course of my research.

The word 'hidden' is not meant to imply that the book will reveal subjects, places or things which are concealed – but a term used to draw attention to subjects and artefacts which do not normally feature in guidebooks, also to curiosities often overlooked on a casual visit to a particular place. My publisher asked me to give due emphasis to 'the nooks and crannies aspect...whilst avoiding undue reliance upon churches and churchyards', but in most villages the church is by far the oldest building and in both counties these contain a wealth of fascinating material. In particular I would mention the churches at Kings Norton, Wistow, Lubenham and Orton-on-the-Hill in Leicestershire, and Brooke, Exton and Stoke Dry in Rutland; but there are so many more. On the other hand I hope that I have not given them 'undue reliance' and, certainly where there was one available, I have left the church guide to tell the story.

Some further comments about churches. First, be cautious in your viewing of lychgates. Some are very old but others are comparatively modern – often erected in memory of a beloved relative. Second, there are some most unusual or rare dedications to be found. St Remigius at Long Clawson and St Egelwin the Martyr (the only one in the country) at Scalford, and several dedicated to St Guthlac are the most obvious. Third, in common with the practice of other works in this series, I have not referred to any articles of portable value in the interiors of churches for obvious reasons. Finally, an unhappy consequence of ever increasing thefts and high-speed getaways is that quite understandably churches are kept locked when not in use – although surprisingly more were found to be open than otherwise. Sadly, on a number of occasions when a church was found to be locked there was absolutely no indication as to where the key could be located.

This book is about villages – the towns have their own guides so are quite able to look after themselves – but although I visited every single village in the two counties, not every one is included in this book because some, however worthy, just did not fit into the requirements of my brief. I was constantly amazed, however, at the sight of so many compact places, often in sight of the nearby town, that still retained (despite the ubiquitous motor-car) the look of a bygone age, refuting the phrase I heard during a 'Thought for the Day' broadcast that 'Villages are becoming housing estates'.

One or two explanatory comments are called for in addition to the Glossary at the end of the book. I have, throughout, kept to the spelling of places used by the Ordnance Survey 'Landranger' maps although some, even fairly recent, books may differ, for example: Lyddington (Rutland) not Liddington, the river Wreake not Wreak, Saxilbye not Saxilby and, of course, Quorn not Quorndon. This is not intended to be a history book – read Arthur Mee's book for the stories of many heroes and personalities in the two counties – but occasionally it was difficult to avoid bringing in a little background material and the people involved. Examples of this are George Fox, the founder of the Quakers, at Fenny Drayton, Lady Jane Grey of Bradgate Park and, of course, Richard III and the Battle of Bosworth – a battle which, in 1485, changed the course of English history.

Jeffery W. Whitelaw
Autumn 1996

ACKNOWLEDGEMENTS

Many guides and church guides were consulted for greater accuracy and I am grateful to the often anonymous writers of these works. I make no apology for occasionally quoting Hoskins, Mee and Pevsner (whose *Buildings of England* series has been my 'bible' and architectural inspiration ever since the books started to be published) and the details are all listed in the Bibliography. To any author who may consider that I have used his words without acknowledgement – sometimes there is only one suitable comment on the feature involved – I offer a humble apology. I am very grateful to all the clergymen, together with scores of other people, who have given of their time to help me in my researches, often making all the difference between success and failure. I thank you all very much.

My publisher has been very patient in allowing me to go beyond his original deadline – I put the blame on my word processor! – but my final apology and grateful thanks must go to my wife who has had to put up with 'I am working on the book' as an excuse for well over a year and whose social life has suffered accordingly. There was no typing to do this time but she helped me with research during the fieldwork and, of course, gave me every encouragement along the way.

HIDDEN
LEICESTERSHIRE

In all the books consulted, only Hoskins makes any reference to the unusual name of *Ab Kettleby*. Listed as 'Chetelbi' in Domesday Book from the original Danish, after Gaufridus Abbe became the owner at the end of the 12th century, the present name (starting as 'Abbe's Ketil's by') gradually evolved. The derivation of this place-name is very unusual: there certainly is no similar type of name in the county but readers may be able to think of others in their own areas.

Driving from Melton Mowbray to Nottingham on the A606 the passing-through driver may think that, apart from the 17th century Sugar Loaf inn on the main road, there is nothing to this place, but the real village stretches westward along the Wartnaby road. Turn off the main road, and almost immediately you pass a thatched ironstone cottage; note that it is single-storeyed with a two-storeyed central bay window. Nearby on the same side of the road is very short Church Lane: it leads nowhere but apart from a walk across a field from Chapel Lane, it is the only approach to St James's church up a track which leads out of it. Overlooking the village pond in Church Lane is the Old Bakehouse and there is the still flowing pyramid-shaped well; spring fed and formerly the only water supply for the village.

In Chapel Lane the Methodist chapel has a plaque on the wall giving its date 'Wesleyan Chapel 1843' and in the middle of the village there is a dovecote in the grounds of the 17th century manor house. St James's church shares a joint ministry with five other churches, and although I visited all these I was unable to gain access to this ironstone building, which is mostly of the 13th century. It has some poppyheaded benches of c1500 and a monument to Everard Digby who died in 1628.

Further westward out of the village is the little hamlet of *Wartnaby* – also listed in Domesday Book – and here is the interesting church of St Michael standing a little apart from the hall and Tower Cottage. This cottage, with its curiously added tower (see *Blaston*) is dated 1656 but Hoskins tells us that 'the rear of the house has substantial remains of a 12th or 13th century building'. The church has an early 13th century south arcade, but the importance lies in the fact that there is still a great deal of the original 13th century ornamental painting – mainly floral with leaves red on white and white on red – in the arches of the arcade. There are some benches of c1500 and outside is a double bellcote very similar to those found on several churches in Rutland.

ANSTEY, GROBY AND RATBY

These three large villages – all virtually within sight of County Hall at Glenfield – are linked together because they are all closely located on the north-west of the city and all have some interesting features to offer.

Anstey was the home of Ned Ludd, a reputedly half-witted lad who in about 1785 smashed the stocking-frames at which he was working. His name was to be adopted during the riots of 1812 when other displaced workers wrecked the newfangled machines introduced by Richard Arkwright and others. This happened long before the housing estates were built and the coming of the motor car; then a much smaller Anstey was grouped around the church, the Nook and Bradgate Road. The Old Hare and Hounds is an old coaching inn right across the road from the church and further up the Bradgate Road is the Congregational church of 1879, now the United Reformed church. Nearby in Park Road is the school house of 1873, now a private dwelling.

In the churchyard of St Mary's church there is a shaft of a 15th century cross near the west tower and gargoyles on all but the east side of the tower under the battlements. Most of the church was rebuilt in the middle of the 19th century but note the south doorway with its crocketed ogee canopy and the dogtoothing on the north doorway. Anstey is best known for its two bridges, both built over the Rothley Brook. The five foot wide five-arched packhorse bridge – dated c1500 although one expert, E. Jervoise, dates it as only late 17th century – can be seen just off the Leicester Road (marked on the Ordnance map) and King William's Bridge – dated late 17th century by the same expert – is at the end of Sheepwash Lane on the way to Castle Hill Country Park.

Groby is a very large village between the A50 and M1 which, in its turn, separates Groby from Ratby. The village has a history right back to the Domesday Book but only in recent times has it grown, with its housing estates, to its present size, so what is hidden in the oldest part? Mention must be made of the Groby Pool on the Newtown Linford road; if Bradgate Park is too much of an effort, here is a quiet and attractive place for a walk with its own car park.

The church of St Philip and St James, which is on the old Markfield Road, was built in 1840 and I will only draw attention to the thin tower. Right next door is the Old Hall with its 15th century tower still standing. There was a castle at Groby which disappeared before the end of the 12th century and Pevsner suggests that the centre of the hall may be part of its outer buildings. The hall became the home of the Greys, and Elizabeth Woodville, wife of Sir John Grey, was living here until she became Edward IV's wife after her husband was killed at St Albans in 1461. A local primary school is named after her.

Across the motorway *Ratby* has already lost one of the earliest railways built in Britain – but the church, also dedicated to St Philip and St James and very prominent on a hill in Church Lane, has interesting features. At the north-east end of the chancel there is a life-sized recumbent effigy in alabaster and black marble inscribed to Henry Sacheverall who died in 1620, and above it is a plaster decoration of a shield of arms c1700. Opposite is a threefold sedilia and a piscina, and the font is of the 14th century. Finally note that the nave has no clerestory and the decoration around the south doorway.

In Church Lane are the 1894 church rooms and Sunday school and, after following the lane down to Chapel Lane, there is a Primitive Methodist chapel. A mile or so to the west of the village is the moated Old Hays Farm of 1733 and Holywell Farm where, at the Holy Well, it is said that the water has never been known to freeze. A walk described in one of the County Council's 'Landmark' pamphlets is routed near both these places and starts from the Ratby memorial – an angel of peace – unveiled by Field Marshal Earl Haig on 13 November 1920 and reproduced on the cover of the pamphlet.

APPLEBY MAGNA AND APPLEBY PARVA

—— These two linked villages, lying just east of the Warwickshire border and the M42 motorway, contain two architectural treasures which have defied time and the developers, and are jealously preserved by generations of local inhabitants. The villages got their name from William de Appleby who originally settled there c1166, and in the chancel of St Michael's church is the tomb together with the alabaster effigies (c1375) of one of his descendants, Sir Edward de Appleby and his wife. There is a full description of the tomb in *Memorials of Old Leicestershire* but I am indebted to the excellent church guide, which also has information about some of the other features of the two villages, for the fact that not only did Sir Edward fight at the Battle of Crecy but that he probably played a great part in the building of the church.

William de Appleby, or one of his descendants, built a stone house surrounded by a moat and entered by a formidable gatehouse. Documents can still be studied concerning the contents of this medieval manor house demolished in the 16th century when the present black and white building was built after the Applebys sold out. What has survived is the gate house itself which even though rebuilt has been, as the WI Village Book says, 'lovingly preserved'. It is now known as the Moat House and is reached via a little path over a stream beside the post office in Mawby's Lane. It is more or less in the centre of the village with one corner of the churchyard actually within a few yards of it and the pathway – described in a little pamphlet outlining *Parish Walks and Rides* in the area.

The church, on the corner of Mawby's Lane and Church

Street, is kept locked but there is a clear indication as to where keys can be obtained with one key held by the author of the guide already mentioned. Because of this guide, I will confine my comments to just one or two important points. Most of the church dates from the 14th century but the box pews and the present west gallery date from 1837. There are remains of some 14th century glass and you will notice, after entering by the west door under the tower, that there are no porches; a south porch and north door went in the 1837 restoration. The north aisle is always associated with the Appleby family and Appleby Magna manor house but the south aisle is connected with the Moore family who became the leading figures in the area after purchasing the manor at Appleby Parva in 1599.

Charles Moore bought the Appleby Parva manor but his second son, Sir John Moore, after a colourful career – particularly during the reign of Charles II – was responsible for the building of Appleby's other treasure, the Appleby Free school which opened in 1697. A complete history of the school (by the author of the church guide) can be obtained at the post office or borrowed from county libraries, so here are just a few facts. Sir John was a friend of Sir Christopher Wren who, in some accounts, has been credited with the design of the building; but although he did approve the design the architect is William Wilson of Leicester. Drive towards Appleby Parva and you will find this unusual building almost midway between the two villages; look through the gateway and marvel that such a fine building has survived for 300 years in the most unlikely of settings. Not only has it survived but since 1956 has flourished as the village primary school bearing Sir John Moore's name in perpetuity.

Appleby Hall, built in Appleby Parva by a descendant in the 18th century, was demolished in the 1920s. Back in Appleby Magna, the almshouses at the top of Mawby's Lane – founded by the Misses Moore in 1839 – have been modernized and elderly folk still live in them. These same Misses Moore gave the church clock in 1850 and, no doubt, had a lot to do with the old National school of 1844 – across the road from the church entrance – now the church hall.

Standing just off the A50 – the old medieval way between Northampton and Leicester – the 1815 tower windmill, which has now been converted into a house, pinpoints the position of *Arnesby* on the map and is a prominent landmark. Around the green off St Peter's Road (which connects the church and the Baptist chapel) are several period houses including Arnesby House, Old Shoulder House and a cruck cottage. On the green is a tree planted in 1973 to commemorate the marriage of Princess Anne and Captain Mark Phillips; another green has an oak planted in 1911 for the coronation of George V. The Baptist chapel, a particularly large one built in 1798 as a successor to the first erected in 1702, now acts as the garage to the manse. Next door to the chapel is The Old Cock, standing at the junction of the A50 with St Peter's Road leading into the village.

Down St Peter's Road are more period houses including The Walnuts with its timbers, and opposite the Old Vicarage which bears the sign of a church. St Peter's church has a great deal of 12th century Norman work in it – particularly both south and north arcades: note the differing capitals. The chancel, the tower and the south aisle itself are of the 14th century. The chancel contains a tomb recess and a double piscina together with a sedilia. Outside is the statue of St Peter under the east gable over the east window.

A mile or two further down, and off, the A50 is *Shearsby*, the origins of which go back to Saxon times. The houses are mainly grouped around the village green and the church of St Mary Magdalene stands on a slight mound on the other side of the narrow road into the village. The old village pump is preserved between Well House and The White House amongst the houses around the green and nearby the old school is now the village hall. Immediately south of the church is the most interesting of the period buildings here; Yeoman Cottage which has the date 1669 on a first floor beam and has been rescued from ruin.

Most of the church was restored by Goddard in the second

part of the 19th century – making the chancel and nave under one roof – but the west tower, with its curious octagon 'cap', is of 1789. However, the medieval piscina and double (originally triple) sedilia remain, together with a screen from Knaptoft church. Note also the crudely sculpted statue of St Mary Magdalene in the sanctuary opposite the piscina, and the carvings on the choir stalls.

South of the village on the Bruntingthorpe Road, the Ordnance map shows 'Bath Hotel and Shearsby Spa' and there the hotel stands on its own. The WI Village Book tells us that apparently in the early part of the 1800s the place was known for its famous salt spring and the hotel was set up so that patrons could 'take the waters' but the project never caught on.

Another mile south, with access gained to it by a little road from the A50, is the deserted village of *Knaptoft* and the ruined church which has been thus since the 17th century. The site has been made into a garden of remembrance, and the earthwork humps and levels of the old village can be seen whilst walking round the well-kept ruin. Outside is another of the plaques put up at historic sites in 1977 to commemorate Queen Elizabeth II's Silver Jubilee (see *Drayton, Hallaton, Kings Norton* and *Medbourne*).

ASFORDBY

—— In 1937 Arthur Mee wrote: 'Nature and Art have both been kind to this village on the Wreake...a charming picture of rural serenity.' The present village hardly measures up to this fulsome praise today. Although less busy because of a bypass it is coupled with Asfordby Hill and Asfordby Valley, and there is the new mine between the A606 and A6006. But the church is a delight and there are other interesting features.

Approaching from Melton Mowbray, take the old road into the village, where, more or less in the middle, is a garage; a necessary and familiar sight in any rural community, but do not despair. Right opposite is an old village cross which stands at what used to be the entrance to Church Lane; this is now blocked off and the approach to All Saints church is made via All Saints Close. Adjacent to the garage is the Jacobean Asfordby Hall, but this looks to be in a sad state of repair. I was told that it is haunted! Just past the hall is the Blue Bell inn with timber in-filling on the east facing wall. Across the road and on the corner of Mill Lane is Wheel Lodge dated 1730. The mill is no more but what was originally a medieval seven foot packhorse bridge – now widened – still carries today's traffic over the river Wreake via the link road to the A607.

And so back to All Saints church. Built of local ironstone in the 13th century, this has a number of interesting features which are not mentioned in the four-page guide. The 14th century tower, with its quatrefoiled-lozenge frieze and gargoyles, is also of flintstone but the spire, a later addition in the 15th century, is of limestone. The north doorway is blocked up but the south doorway is a fine example of 14th century work with ballflower decoration. All the old guide books mention a Saxon sculptured stone on the outer wall of the north transept; this, when removed in 1961 along with others, was found to be a pre-Conquest cross shaft. The three parts are now on display inside the church, at the west end of the south aisle.

There is a piscina in the north transept and another one in the south transept, but in the chancel is not only an ogee-headed piscina and three-seated sedilia but also, opposite, a two-tiered aumbry. The screen is basically 15th century although the figures are modern, and above the south end note the possible remains of a rood stairway. At the west end of the church is an old clock face dated 1824 with only a single hand bearing the initials of two churchwardens of the time. Before you leave, look upwards to the clerestory windows. The 15th century roof is supported by twelve wooden angels – five on each side supported in turn by grotesquely-faced corbels whilst the sixth pair opposite each other at the west end, are on plain corbels.

Ashby Folville was listed in Domesday as 'Ascbi' (the place by the ash trees), then about 1200 'Foleville' was added (held by the Folvilles). Although this tiny hamlet can be driven through very quickly, stop to admire the many treasures in St Mary's church. First, note the Carington Arms inn with its coat-of-arms sign and, not quite opposite the church, the unusual Wooton Cottages built in 1906 with overhanging decorative woodwork. The manor house (no longer owned by the Smith-Caringtons) was rebuilt by John Ely between 1891 and 1893, and Ely was also responsible for a great deal of restoration in the church between 1885 and 1913 – commissioned by Herbert Smith-Carington.

For such a small place the church is impressive, and as a very full guide has been written by Wing Commander J.H. Carington-Smith, I will just draw attention to a few particular features. In the Carington chapel a stone effigy of Sir Eustace de Folville is amongst the later Smith tombs. Note the piece of iron in the side of the effigy, apparently to represent the lance with which he was killed in a duel in 1347. There is a rare hourglass holder behind the pulpit but on no account miss the roof of the nave. There is a carved and painted angel choir on grotesque corbels – most of the angels are playing musical instruments, with one playing bagpipes – and more carvings of faces or creatures in the centre.

Leaving the village past the Carington Arms head for *Barsby*, a mile or so away, and on the way pass the old school of 1849 with its attractive exterior. Despite 'Church Lane', there is no church in Barsby but the village is of particular interest because of the variety of cottages – some dated. At the crossroads turn right, and on the left is a cottage with 1701 picked out in brick. Further along is one dated 1691 (and this has a fire insurance mark above a blocked-up window) and opposite is one with the builder's initials and dated 1707.

Back across the Ashby Folville to South Croxton Road to what is called Baggrave End there are more curiosities, and none more so than Godson's Folly in Church Lane. Apparently the building was intended as a chapel mortuary and built in the shape of a church, but was never consecrated. Also in Baggrave End is The Old Bakehouse, a cottage opposite the end of Church Lane called Three Bows (because it has three bow windows) and, on the corner of the crossroads, a former Wesleyan chapel which is now a private dwelling.

After seeing Baggrave End, and continuing southward to *South Croxton* (pronounced 'Croson'), it is somewhat surprising to see St John the Baptist church at the top of quite an unexpected hill with the small village trailing away down the hillside. Halfway down on the left-hand side note Malt Shovel Cottage; intrigued by this name I discovered that the place used to be an inn. Apart from the church, and immediately north of it the most important feature here is the moated site. Though marked on the Ordnance map nothing remains to indicate the nature of the building.

As you enter the church, notice first the stone memorial surmounted by a lamp which illuminates the path into the porch. This was donated by the Sunday school to commemorate the completion of repairs to the tower which was extensively damaged by lightning in 1936. Inside, the tub-shaped font is Norman decorated with curious figures and interlaced arches, and in the roof of the nave above the corbels are more figures (five each side) holding shields. Outside note that the repaired tower is of ironstone but the short spire is of limestone.

ASHBY PARVA AND ULLESTHORPE

Situated between Leire and Bitteswell, *Ashby Parva* can boast of several interesting farmhouses and the old school of 1832 which became the village hall in 1968. This has a plaque recording that it was 'Built and Endowed by Sarah Bowyer from a bequest made to her for charitable purposes by Lucy Goodacre, widow of Thomas Goodacre, Gent, of Leire'. The old school stands between Orpudds Farm (1695) and The

Hollybush, and opposite the church is the 1765 Longacres Farm.

St Peter's church is mainly of the 15th century and, because the south wall of the nave – there are no aisles – appears to have been built out further south, the nave is not symmetrical with the tower and the chancel. The chancel and the porch were rebuilt in 1866 but the font is Norman and there are the remains of a rood loft stairway. Outside, note the two faces on the north wall of the tower below the battlements.

Ashby Parva is in the same group of parishes as *Leire*, whereas *Ullesthorpe* is in the Claybrooke parish but I have linked them firstly because of geographic convenience, and secondly because the WI Village Book tells us that 'Ullesthorpe is also reputed to be the home of Leicester cheese. It is believed that Mr Tomlinson made the cheese first in Ashby Parva, later moving to Ullesthorpe.'

No parish church here but there is a large Congregational chapel which was built in 1825. Twenty-five years earlier the brick tower windmill was built and this dominates the village.

BAGWORTH, BARLESTONE AND THORNTON

——— A trio of former mining villages which might at first sight seem to have very little to offer to qualify for the label of 'hidden' but, as is so often the case, there are a few compensations. At *Bagworth* Holy Rood church stands at the end of Old School Lane. This modern (prefabricated?) building was built on the site of the 1873 church (which had a medieval tower) demolished in 1968. A Norman arch survives and you will see that it has been built into the modern structure. Like the original church, the old school itself had also to be closed due to subsidence.

At *Barlestone* the church of St Giles was, except for the chancel, entirely rebuilt in 1855 and a lot of the medieval masonry was utilised in the work. To the north-east of the church note Church Farm, which is of the early 18th century.

A memorial and reminder of the past history of the area – something which I have found elsewhere locally – is a pit-head winding wheel set in concrete at the beginning of the Barton-in-the-Beans road.

Half way along the road to *Thornton* from Bagworth, by the discontinued railway line, is an isolated Baptist chapel of 1885 and on the edge of the village is a house dated 1700. Thornton has been called 'ugly' but the attractively-shaped reservoir and the church of St Peter on its western shore go a long way to redeem the village. The reservoir was constructed in 1853 and was the first built for the express purpose of supplying Leicester with water. Larger and more modern ones have taken over this function and Thornton's 'lake' is used now for pleasure only.

The key of St Peter's church is kept at the shop on the corner. St Peter's has an early 14th century inner door which is reputed to have come from the ruined priory at Ulverscroft; it is massive with the remains of contemporary or even 13th century metal work. Inside note the coat of arms of George IV on the north wall of the nave, and the curious triangular window at the end of the north aisle. Great survivors here are the base of a rood screen of circa 1500 – almost destroyed by Cromwell's soldiers – and a complete set of bench ends of circa 1560. A last look down the nave will reveal a tympanum, with the Ten Commandments and other texts, acting as the chancel arch.

BARROW - UPON - SOAR

Barrow may not be the most exciting of villages, but there is a small area near the church worthy of attention. On the corner of Church Street and Beveridge Street, its heavy pedimented gateway immediately opposite the lychgate of the church, is the Old Men's Hospital. Completed in 1694 it was built by Humphrey Babington in memory of his uncle Theophilus Cave, who died in 1656. There is information about the foundation on two large boards in the church, which also has a tablet to Cave in the chancel. Nearby is the

St. John the Baptist church, Belton.

Old Women's Hospital, built in 1825 as a foundation of the men's hospital.

On the other corner of Beveridge Street, in Church Gate, is a well preserved octagonal lock-up of 1827 with a pyramidal roof. In Beveridge Street is the house where William Beveridge, later Bishop of St Aspath, was born in 1636. Here also is the Baptist church with various commemorative stones on the wall: 'Built 1822' and 'Rebuilt 1926'.

Holy Trinity church has the usual pinnacles, gargoyles and frieze on the tower to be found in this area and there are more gargoyles not only on the nave exterior but also on the south doorway. Note also the elaborate tomb monument to John Beaumont and a very old gravestone, dated either 1601 or 1691, both very near to the doorway. The sedilia, piscina and reredos are all fairly modern (circa 1890) in a Victorian chancel, but note the angels in the nave roof and the monument to Martha Utber who died in 1745, in the south transept.

 BELTON AND OSGATHORPE

———— The A512 road runs between Loughborough and Ashby-de-la-Zouch. Just before you reach Thringstone, you suddenly come upon what the poet Wordsworth called 'the ivied ruins of forlorn Grace Dieu'. Grace Dieu Priory, suppressed in 1536 by Henry VIII, was founded by Lady Roesia Grace de Verdun circa 1240 and after her death she was entombed at the priory. At the dissolution the tomb was brought to Belton and can be found in the north-west corner of St John the Baptist church. This beautiful alabaster effigy of Lady Roesia is a genuine 13th century figure – proved by the wimple, according to Pevsner – although there is doubt about the age of some of the other figures around the tomb.

The village is reached by one of two minor roads from the A512 and the more easterly one goes past what is marked on the OS map as an 'Earthwork'. The *Memorials* book points out that, in Celtic or Roman times, it would have been just a simple defended enclosure. The church stands in the middle and at the highest point of the village, at one end of a large market place in which there is one of the country's few permanent maypoles, surmounted by a fox. The present pole dates only from 1952 – an earlier one was knocked down by a bus!

A History of the Church and Village of Belton by Anne Tarver is available in the church, an excellent guide which not only gives you a tour of the church but also provides a fairly comprehensive history of this and the local community. I will, however, pick out one reference which will explain why Belton and Osgathorpe have been linked together. At the west end of the north aisle there is a brass plate recording the bequest of Mrs Margaret Mead 'who left land in both parishes, the profits from which were to be used to buy two shillings worth of bread every week in perpetuity' also 'A further £10 was to be given alternately to Belton, Osgathorpe and Thringstone for the apprenticeship of a poor boy to a trade anywhere in the country.'

A mile or so along the B5324 a minor road leads you into *Osgathorpe*, a small hamlet with a history which, through its very name, can be linked to the Danish occupation at the end of the 9th century. Here, too, hidden away as in Appleby, are two more of the county's architectural gems.

St Mary's church was restored in Victorian times when an apse was added and there were further additions in 1931 but basically it is of the 14th century. The most remarkable detail of the original building is a squint; a square window on the south side set diagonally so as to allow a view of the altar. In the churchyard there is a five-sided sundial and right next to the church is Manor Farm, a Tudor timber-framed farmhouse which is one of the oldest in the village with an old pump in the garden.

Opposite the church, on the other side of Church Lane and at right-angles to the road, is The Residence which was originally an almshouse for clergymen's widows. Both this building and the old grammar school in Church Lane were built in 1670 helped by a bequest from Thomas Harley, a former Lord Mayor of London whose name is perpetuated in

Harley House. The old grammar school is now the village hall: note the elaborate inscription over the entrance.

BILLESDON AND SKEFFINGTON

These villages are linked together here for three reasons: they lie on either side of the Melton Mowbray to Market Harborough road, both have now been bypassed by the A47 – whereas the road once passed through them – and they are linked through the Fernie Hunt. The Billesdon Hunt was founded in 1838, a gentleman from Skeffington later kept a pack of hounds at Billesdon and, when Charles Fernie became MOH in 1888, the hunt changed its name.

Billesdon (shown in Domesday Book with an 'e') has a long history which probably starts with Bronze Age man using the nearby high ground of what is now called Billesdon Coplow and later, when early British settlers moved on to the hill, the very name of the village undoubtedly derived from the fact that it must have been 'Bill's Hill'. Later there is evidence that the Anglo-Saxons settled in the valley where the village now stands: a 6th century Anglo-Saxon brooch was found at the site of a burial mound near the village.

The road through the village is called Uppingham Road – a relic from the time before the bypass. No 1 has been restored by the Leicestershire Historic Buildings Trust; there is a sundial over the front doorway. Nearby is the village green on which stands the war memorial and the base and shaft of an old village cross. Most of the houses along the old main road are of brick but those in the older part of the village clustered around the church are of limestone.

St John the Baptist church provides a good guide for a very modest fee so I will just say that, whilst most of the church only dates from the middle of the 19th century, the north arcade and the base of the tower were built early in the 13th century; the font is of the same period. On the edge of the churchyard is Billesdon's most precious relic – a school founded, or possibly refounded, in 1650. The building was probably already a school before William Sharpe set up his

'Free School' in 1650 and a plaque on the wall tells us that George Fox, the founder of the Society of Friends, and George Villiers, 1st Duke of Buckingham (who was assassinated in 1628), both started their education in the former school. I mentioned that there was a sundial over the door on the house in Uppingham Road but this old school has no less than four – one on each of the four walls!

The WI Village Book tells us that there was a settlement in *Skeffington* before the Norman Conquest, and certainly in Domesday Book it is shown as 'Sciftitone'. The story of this village, until recent times, has been dominated over the centuries by the Skeffington family. They lived in the hall and were buried in the nearby church dedicated to St Thomas à Becket. The extensively embattled hall, a private residence, can be viewed from the little road leading off the A47 and through the village. Unfortunately the church is kept locked and there is no indication as to who holds the keys.

BLASTON AND HORNINGHOLD

I have linked these disparate villages together largely because of the Reverend Humfrey Michel, the controversial rector of the two places. Unbeknown to his parishioners, he kept very critical records of all their shortcomings and his diary is full of 'quaint grumbles'. Arthur Mee tells us that, as late as 1702, he was still crying out against the 'murderers of King Charles the martyr' and that right up to his death he was still grumbling about the people of Horninghold – so much so that he elected to be buried at Blaston!

Blaston, known by this name as early as the Domesday Book, is a small one-street village. As you approach from the east, St Giles church, in which Humfrey Michel was buried in November 1722, can be seen at the other end. There are a number of interesting buildings in the street, the Clocktower House with its decorated front door being the most prominent. Opposite are two attractive ironstone houses and, at the church end of the street, a thatched house bearing a plaque '1647, Restored 1907'.

Just round the corner, at the start of a gated road to Medbourne, St Giles stands looking rather forlorn on a small rectangular plot. Strangely, for such a small place, there are two churches here. St Giles was rebuilt in 1878 – very small with nave and chancel all in one, plus an apse and a bell turret. Somewhat earlier the other church, St Michael's, was also rebuilt, in 1867, but is now derelict.

There was a Norman settlement at *Horninghold*, a couple of miles to the north. It was Horniwale in Domesday Book, but only St Peter's church gives any indication of the connection. This is virtually another one-street village, but quite a different place to Blaston, due to the efforts of a prosperous farmer, Thomas Hardcastle, who in the early years of this century turned the place into a garden village. As one author writes: 'Overall the village has an air of quiet and mellow prosperity'. A small neat village green with an oak village sign and the prosperous well-kept houses, mostly 20th century, positively preclude anything 'hidden', so that leaves the church which three writers have described as having been 'conservatively', 'sensitively' and 'skilfully' restored by Victorian craftsmen.

Entry is by the north door but the south door, no longer in use, helps the dating of the Norman antiquity of the church; chancel, nave and west tower were built circa 1150. There is a Knight Templar coffin lid of approximately 1260 and an octagonal font on legs. The altar rails are 18th century but the most interesting features are the eight medieval bench-ends – some with poppyheads – at the rear of the church.

BOTTESFORD AND MUSTON

—— Except for a little hamlet north of the railway level crossing, the large village of Bottesford is the most northerly in the county. Because of its nearness to Belvoir Castle, it has many links with the Earls of Rutland – indicated by the monuments in the chancel of St Mary's church which, as Hoskins says, is 'the glory of the place'. But first, the village with its cross at the centre and some old stocks. Down

Church Street is Rectory Court, reputedly built in 1708 and enlarged in 1789. On the wall facing the road there are stone plaques and a coat of arms from the old school house dated 1732 which used to stand in the churchyard and another stating that it existed 1732–1855. In Market Street are Fleming's almshouses of 1620; Samuel Fleming was the rector who, having been nearly drowned on one occasion when crossing the river Devon which flows by the south entrance to the churchyard, had a narrow footbridge built some time between 1581 and 1620 so that 'for the future no man should there run the same risque'.

On the other side of the churchyard and very near to the west tower of the church is Providence Cottage with the date 1731 picked out in brick. Opposite is the Earl of Rutland's hospital founded about 1590. Devon Lane runs alongside the river, and after passing a house dated 1621 you must take care – a ford divides the lane in two! You can either drive through or retrace your steps to approach the other side from the south. Whatever you do, the Methodist church is on the south side of the ford and further down is the old Wesleyan chapel of 1845, now a private house.

St Mary's church is not only one of the largest village churches in England but also most notable for the remarkable collection of tombs in the chancel – some from medieval times but particularly those of successive Earls of Rutland of Belvoir Castle. An admirable illustrated guide is available to the church and its monuments so I will just point out a few features which might be missed because of the chancel. Formerly in the chancel, note the four hatchments on the wall of the north aisle and another on the south aisle. Several of the county's churches have the coats of arms of Georgian monarchs; here, above the chancel arch and carved in elm and plaster, are the arms of Queen Victoria. More impor-tantly, above the arms, though a little difficult to see, are the remnants of a medieval 'Doom' painting. Note also what is left of the 15th century newel-stairway to the now vanished rood loft just west of the chancel arch. Finally, look upwards in the nave at the 14 corbels supporting the roof, and at the animal carvings above the pillars.

Lying just south of the A52 trunk road, and a mile or so to the east of Bottesford, is the village of *Muston* where a complete village cross – rebuilt to mark the coronation of George V – stands on the village green in Woolsthorpe Lane. The poet George Crabbe was appointed rector of St John the Baptist church in 1789 and moved on to Trowbridge after the death of his wife Sarah, to whom there is a tablet in the church. She died in 1813 after a long bout of 'melancholy' following the death of five of their seven children. In the church the screen and pulpit are of the 17th century but there are some ancient benches with poppyheads.

BREEDON-ON-THE-HILL AND STAUNTON HAROLD

—— Many of the present-day village names of British origin derive from the natural features in the vicinity – rivers, hills or forests – used by the Anglo-Saxons and later given to the villages which grew up in the neighbourhood. Thus, according to A.H. Smith's *English Place-Name Elements*, the word 'Breedon' is made up of two words – the Early British or Celtic word 'Bre' meaning a hill and the Old English word 'don' also meaning a hill or fort. 'On-the-Hill' – added at an unknown later date – is, therefore, a quite unnecessary triplication which was probably tacked on when the original derivation had been forgotten.

The hill is certainly the dominant feature in an otherwise fairly flat area and can be seen – with the church of St Mary and St Hardulph very prominent on the summit – from many miles away in every direction. Because of its lofty position, the Iron Age inhabitants fortified it at some time between the third and first centuries BC (expert opinion differs!) and the remains of the ramparts of this hill-fort are to the west of the church. During excavations in 1946, when archaeologists estimated that the fort was in use until the middle of the first century AD, Iron Age pottery and tools were discovered; these are now in a Leicester museum.

At the foot of the hill, the village – long harassed by traffic

Holy Trinity church, Staunton Harold.

through its narrow winding high street and the huge limestone quarry eating into the side of the hill – now has a bypass, so it is somewhat easier (and safer) to investigate before returning back up the hill to the church and what Pevsner calls the 'fortunate survival' of Saxon sculpture of 'a style different from anything existing on the Continent of Europe'.

At the eastern end of the village – near to where the lorries enter the quarry workings and right by the road – is a small landscaped garden. Probably it would go unnoticed except for the fact that it is entered by what can only be called a miniature folly. A twin-towered stone structure, each tower with a castellated top and their two bases forming an unusual archway (with another half-moon opening above) leads to steps built up into this little embellishment welcoming you to the village. I have no other details but what an imaginative idea! It certainly helps you to forget the ugly scar of the quarry just behind you.

In the middle of the village stands a rare survival of the 18th century, a relic of the days before there was an organised police force – the village lock-up. It has a conical roof and a stout nail-studded door and unusually adjoins the roadway, not on the village green where they are normally found. On the little green, at the west end of the village, there is an unusually shaped war memorial recording the names of the villagers who gave their lives in the two world wars. Built of stone it neatly complements the other two small buildings described above.

When you return to the church by the road from the war memorial and go to view the renowned Saxon sculpture, I suggest that you purchase the illustrated guide which, together with full details in the nave, will help you to marvel at the more than 70 feet of carved friezes of the eighth and ninth centuries far better than I can here. There was a monastery on the site in the eighth century which was later sacked by the Danes, then about 1120 Robert de Ferrers founded an Augustinian priory which was a victim of the Dissolution. However, the Shirley family who succeeded the Ferrers and were established at Staunton Harold by 1423 managed to retain the tower and chancel of the old priory church and these remains became the parish church. The sculpture, as Arthur Mee says 'by some miraculous good fortune' remained and the Shirley family claimed the north aisle as their own. Today Shirley tombs and the almost totally enclosed Shirley pew of 1627 can still be seen; the main nave seating is 18th century box pews.

Staunton Harold Hall, now a Sue Ryder hospice, is four miles away. Perhaps Sir Robert Shirley thought that distance too far to go to church, for in 1653 he built Holy Trinity church in the grounds. It is unique in that it survives as the only complete church built during the Commonwealth. An ardent Royalist, Sir Robert was put to death in the Tower by Cromwell and is now buried in the church. Holy Trinity, with its box pews, oak and wrought-iron screens, and painted ceiling, is now in the care of the National Trust and open to view usually between April and October.

BROUGHTON ASTLEY, SAPCOTE AND STONEY STANTON

―――― Not much is hidden in the large industrial village of *Broughton Astley* but it is included because of its two churches – the parish church of St Mary and the Baptist chapel – and because it was here that George Fox (see *Fenny Drayton*) addressed his first great outdoor meeting in 1647. He distrusted churches, calling them 'steeple houses', and it is believed that he preached near where the bridges cross the stream on the way in to the church.

St Mary's is mainly of the 14th century, with the chancel of the 13th century, albeit largely rebuilt in 1882. Actually, the church has a two-naved appearance because the north aisle is as wide and as high as the nave. Only two of the octagonal piers of the aisle have decorated capitals – the other two are plain. The pulpit is of the 18th century, some grotesque corbel faces in the nave are 15th century but the most ancient treasure here is the Norman piscina, or possibly a stoup, on a pillar carved with zigzag standing by the entrance door.

Once a separate village, Sutton-in-the-Elms is now just part of Broughton Astley at its northern end and noted for its Baptist chapel which stands just off the B581. Founded originally in 1650, the present building was built in 1815 but with an apse added in 1907.

Moving on westward across the Fosse Way you come to the two villages of *Sapcote* and *Stoney Stanton* – linked over the years because of quarrying. This may have ceased but Stoney Cove, made up of two old worked-out quarries and about midway between the two villages, has become nationally known as a popular water sports centre and particularly as an inland diving centre. I was unable to discover the whereabouts of the key holders of either of the parish churches so can only say that All Saints at Sapcote is of the 14th century, with much restorative work in 1843, and that St Michael's church at Stoney Stanton, again heavily Victorianised, has, according to Hoskins, only one feature of interest: the Norman tympanum which is now over the doorway of the vestry.

East of the church in Sapcote are some almshouses of 1847 and in the main street is the old school of 1819. Not actually a pretty village, Stoney Stanton has, however, several attractive points of interest. The Methodist church, wedged between two houses, is still flourishing and there are two period houses to note: a brick and timber house on Carey Hill and in Long Street Yew Tree House stands out. In its time it has been the village school and the post office.

BUCKMINSTER AND SEWSTERN

In *Buckminster* the visitor's first impressions are of tree-lined streets and how different the village looks in comparison with most others in the county: as Hoskins says 'an estate village with the air of Victorian opulence'. The hall of the Dysart family was demolished in 1952 although the 19th century stables still remain. There is a large green with the church to the north of it, and to the south is a terrace of 16 gabled 19th century cottages.

St John the Baptist church is unusual in that the tower is at the east end of the short south aisle, and in the south-east corner of the nave by the chancel arch there is an octagonal newel staircase to the tower and the former rood loft. The large painting of *The Adoration of the Magi* came from Alton Towers in Staffordshire. This is on the north wall of the north aisle; high above, note also the two tiers of heads under the rafters. There is a similar arrangement in the south aisle and, in the nave, another nine corbels making a total of some 40 faces which are, as Arthur Mee memorably points out 'looking from the walls as from a medieval picture book'. In the chancel note the double piscina and the triple stepped sedilia with a recess opposite, and the curious recess – possibly a blocked doorway – behind the altar.

Outside again, note the three niches on the porch above the entrance and a sundial on a buttress on the tower. There are as is often the case, more heads to be found on the exterior mouldings of various windows. In the churchyard is a not very attractive large mausoleum of the Dysart family dating from circa 1875.

Sewstern and Buckminster are in one parish (together with Coston and Garthorpe). The Ordnance map shows that Sewstern is right on the Lincolnshire border, seemingly the planners or cartographers have gone out of their way to make sure that the whole of the village is in the county. The boundary line runs along the old medieval, or even earlier, salt road known as Sewstern Lane or the Viking Way but there is a definite kink in it around the east of the village!

A large building dated 1752 in the Main Street is now split into two houses, and nearby is the Wesleyan church of 1903. Down a little lane opposite the Blue Dog inn is Holy Trinity church, a chapel of ease, which has an 1842 bellcote built in a neo-Norman style. Probably the most interesting thing here is an old AA sign giving the name of the village and distances to Stamford, Grantham and London, affixed to the wall of the Blue Dog inn. Before the Second World War, these round signs were seen everywhere but they were all removed when invasion was feared in 1940. I am informed by the AA Archives officer of their Public Relations department that they know of some 100 others in the country but that, apart from one in the Leicester museum, this at Sewstern is the only one in the county.

 ## BURROUGH - ON - THE - HILL

—— Between Somerby and the village of Burrough-on-the-Hill is Burrough Hill itself, some 700 feet above sea level with an Iron Age fort at the summit. There is a spacious car park, and the fort is open in daylight hours throughout the year. The village, despite its title, lies south-west of the hill and has a history possibly going back to well before Roman times. It certainly had the name 'Burg' in 1086 when Domesday Book was being completed. More recent history centres round Burrough Court – burnt down during the Second World War – because it was here that Edward, Prince of Wales as he was then, first met Mrs Wallis Simpson. Today the Burrough House Gardens are advertised as open at certain times and the Bower House, originally sited at Burrough Court and where this historic meeting took place, is one of the attractions.

Burrough House lies south of a bend in the road and across from it is a preserved village pump. Back up the Main Street are several interesting houses with Manor House, a large brick house dated 1781, opposite the church as the most imposing. Note Brasenose Cottages (No 40) next door with Brasenose College, Oxford, with the College arms over the doorway. They were built in 1909 to celebrate 400 years of the college, founded in 1509 by Sir Richard Sutton, the squire of Burrough. Further south, on the same side of the road, is Gartree Cottage dated 1815, the year of Waterloo. Opposite is an ironstone building and nearer to the church is the impressive Old Rectory, now privately owned. North of the church are two old buildings up Spring Lane – The Limes of 1752 and Cheselden (or Cheseldyne) Farm dating back to sometime in the 17th century.

At St Mary's church there is a ten-page guide (with some very useful line drawings of the font, corbel faces and the two halves of the split tomb chest of William Stockton and his wife) so I will only presume to add just an odd note or two.

As you enter the churchyard by the gate opposite the manor house, you will see at once the headstones – 'in reluctant line like conscripts' according to the guide – and many are worth studying for the decorative inscriptions. The guide mentions that the tower and spire were rebuilt in 1878, but note also that the clock – dedicated as a memorial to the Burnaby family – must have been erected at the same time. Finally, as a Second World War soldier myself, I was particularly interested in the two sets of medals displayed in the south aisle with the memorials of two local worthies: Sir Raymond Greene who lived at Burrough House, and Frederick Gerald Peake who served under Lawrence of Arabia in the First World War, and was later to raise and command the Arab Legion.

BURTON LAZARS

—— When approached from the direction of Oakham along the A606 this village, only 'Burtone' in Domesday Book, looks from afar as if it were strung out just below the last ridge before entering Melton Mowbray. It owes its present unusual name and prominence to just one fact. A monastic leper hospital (the old name was 'Lazar' from Lazarus of the Bible story) was founded here in the 12th century by Robert de Mowbray for The Order of St Lazarus of Jerusalem and, according to *Memorials of Old Leicestershire* it became 'the chief of all the lazar houses in England, and subject only to the great house in Jerusalem...A spring of repute was the cause of the foundation at Burton'. Although the hospital ceased to operate in 1544 soon after the dissolution of the monasteries, the spring was utilised as a bath and drinking-well as late as the 18th century.

After turning left into Lime Street at the southern end of the village, a right fork ends at a farm gate after passing Peppers Farm and Hall Farm. Walk to another gate with a

William Squire monument, Burton Lazars.

Countryside Commission sign and on the other side the
layout of the hospital with its hollows, mounds and
waterways for curative bathing etc. can still be made out.
Back to the main road and on the corner of Cross Lane, the
second turning right, is the mainly 13th century St James'
church.

The most obvious feature here is what every passing
motorist cannot fail to see when driving past the churchyard
along this western edge of the village – the 20 foot high
monument of a weaver William Squire who died towards the
end of the 18th century: a visitor to the church will see that it
is adorned with skulls, serpents, eagles and the figures of
Time, Faith, Hope and Charity. Near the porch is the base of
the old village cross, and the exterior of the church, as the
guide says, 'is distinguished by its unusual bell-turret

containing two bells' but, unlike those bellcotes in Rutland, it has a little saddle-back tower topped by a short spire. I will let the guide tell the rest of the story of this mainly 13th century church but on no account miss the ten carved 15th century wooden minstrels – each on a grotesque corbel – together supporting the nave roof and forming a whole orchestra of period instruments.

BURTON ON THE WOLDS AND PRESTWOLD

Stand in the centre of *Burton* near the 'K' type pillar box and you think that the B676 road which runs through it is unlimited – the traffic does tend to speed past. Nevertheless, within a few hundred yards you will come upon some interesting features even though much of the village is made up of modern commuter dwellings.

Across the road from the pillar box is what was originally the lodge at the entrance to Burton Hall. Now it is a private house at the end of Hall Drive leading to houses built in the former grounds of the hall which since 1965 has been a nursing home. A few yards from the old lodge and set into the wall is a well with constant running water; originally this was the only source of water in the village until about 1947 when piped water was installed. There is no Anglican church in the village but the Methodist church, with a stone plaque bearing the legend 'Wesleyan Chapel MDCCCXLVI', prominent on the outside wall, is still active.

I was told that, today, Anglicans go to Wymeswold church but at some period in the last century they were assigned special seats in St Andrew's church at *Prestwold*, a mile or so distant. The village has long disappeared, and the church remains in the grounds of Prestwold Hall which is now a conference centre. Enter the grounds from the Hoton Road past two lodges with Doric colonnades and obtain the key of the church at the Hall, not failing to look at the beautifully painted ceiling in the entrance hall.

The church was extensively restored at the end of the 19th century by Sir Arthur Blomfield; there is little of interest in the nave except two hatchments and an old musical instrument hanging on the north wall. Sir Christopher Packe, a strong supporter of Cromwell, bought the estate in 1650 and the chancel is full of Packe monuments and, even more interestingly, of their predecessors. On the south side of the altar is an elaborate tomb, erected in 1631, to Sir William Skipwith who has his sword by his side and 15 cherubic angels in an arch keeping watch over him and his wife whose effigy is a little lower. On the north side of the altar is an alabaster tomb chest of late 15th century and a similar one nearby circa 1520: note the carvings of bedesmen around the base of both. Sir Christopher has his own standing wall-monument with his effigy in a semi-reclining pose and opposite there is a memorial to Major Robert Packe who was killed at the Battle of Waterloo ('his remains lie buried there'). There are other memorials to the Packes but I must not omit the sad sculpted figure (by Richard Westmacott) of Charles Hussey Packe who died in 1842 whilst still a schoolboy at Eton.

CADEBY, MARKET BOSWORTH, SHENTON AND SUTTON CHENEY

The decisive battle of the Wars of the Roses on 22nd August 1485, known as Bosworth Field, was actually fought in the parish of Sutton Cheney, but it was named after the better known landmark of Market Bosworth and so, with Cadeby and Shenton situated very near the battlefield, these four places are inevitably linked together. *Cadeby* is little more than a hamlet but the church is mainly 14th century. South of the church is Jasmine Cottage with a plaque on it which reads: 'Erected AD 1865 on a site given by Revd R.T. Adnutt MA to the successive rectors and churchwardens of Cadeby for a school house'. In Wood Lane is the timber-framed Church Cottage which is on record as being there in 1582.

In so small a place, I was pleased to find that All Saints church had a guide so will only add a comment or two. From the guide it is clear that Cadeby is a brass rubbing centre, not mentioned is the scratch dial on the south-east buttress of the south aisle. Inside there is no chancel arch and, outside, the bellcote, with its pyramid top, was only built in 1843; it is quite unlike those medieval bellcotes to be found in Rutland. The large building with many chimneys to the west of the church is the old rectory.

Southward to the slightly larger village of *Sutton Cheney* which, according to the church guide, has been an equal partner with the parish of Cadeby since 1923. However, because of its history and nearness to the Bosworth Battlefield visitor centre, St James's, signposted as 'The Battlefield Church', must attract many more visitors than its neighbour, though the church guide stresses that the battle actually took place in the parish of Sutton Cheney. On entering the village you pass the large building now called Hall Farm which dates from the early 17th century. Pevsner tells us that the dates 1601, 1612 and 1656 can be seen in different places in the building. Immediately east of the church are the former almshouses founded in 1612 by Sir William Roberts. The Almshouse is now a very thriving restaurant.

Tradition has it that Richard III attended his last Mass in what is now known as the Battlefield Church and it is full of memorabilia of the last of the Plantagenets, including a brass memorial to the king erected by the Richard the Third Society in 1968, and the Society was also responsible for the kneelers in the pews, some of which are 17th century box pews: all are devoted to Richard III and many have his motto on them 'Loyaulte Me Lie' (Loyalty Binds Me).

Sir William Roberts, who died in 1633, lies in his alabaster tomb on the north side of the chancel and above him, in a mural monument, are his two wives kneeling at desks facing one another. A drawing of his tomb is on the back of the four-page guide.

The Bosworth Battlefield visitor centre is off the Sutton Cheney to Shenton road and is clearly signposted. As the advertising brochure says, you can 'roam the Battle Trails, experience medieval times in the extensive Visitor Centre, and re-live that fateful day, on the site of Bosworth Field'. On the western edge of the Battle Trail Walk is Shenton Station,

King Richard's Well, Bosworth Field.

the terminus of what is known as The Battlefield Line, on
which steam trains run from here to Shackerstone on what is,
in the main, a dismantled railway. Across the Ashby-de-la-
Zouch Canal is the village of *Shenton* itself, near where Henry
Tudor, the future Henry VII, positioned his forces before the
battle. The present church was built in 1862 to replace an
earlier building on the same site but it contains a fine marble
memorial to William Wollaston, who died in 1666, and his
wife. He it was who built Shenton Hall in 1629 but only the
gatehouse and the north-west front are of that date. There is
a dovecote of 1769, complete with a potence (revolving
ladder), which can be found near the stables.

    And so on to the small market town of *Market Bosworth*,
standing some two or three miles north of the battlefield and

where the spire of St Peter's church would have been visible to anyone who had time to look northward on that historic day. All roads lead to the market place – there has been a market here on Wednesdays since 1285 – but parking is difficult at any time whether it is Market Day or not! Right by the market place and at the beginning of the road to the station on the Battlefield Line is the Dixie Grammar School built in 1836 in a Tudor style: the Wolstan Preparatory School for four to nine year olds is also in the building. Further down that road is the façade of the former 1836 workhouse which has been preserved in a block of town houses. On the other side of the market place is a row of timber-framed and thatched cottages opposite the Midland Bank. Down Main Street is the Free Church (United Reformed) of 1848 and practically opposite is Church Street and the approach to St Peter's where there are riches indeed waiting for the visitor on which I need not comment; there is not only a brief guide but also an illustrated church trail!

Finally, Market Bosworth Hall, dating from the end of the 17th century and at one time a hospital, is now a luxury hotel but, after finding somewhere to leave the car in the car park of the country park, look to your right and you will see the exterior of the walled garden of the hall and the three-storeyed Italianate belvedere tower which is the centrepiece of the visible wall.

CASTLE DONINGTON

During the Second World War an airstrip between Diseworth and Castle Donington was known as RAF Diseworth. Initially the first civil development was conveniently named after the nearest town, Castle Donington; that small wartime airstrip has now become the East Midlands International Airport. But, long before the advent of the noise in the sky, motor-cycle racing and then car-racing took place in what had been the park of Donington Hall. The name of the town, therefore, was already well known and even more so after the first British Grand Prix was staged there in 1937.

The hall, built by William Wilkins, the architect responsible for the National Gallery, is now owned by British Midland Airways but there are remains of lodges at the approaches to the race circuit and to what is described in the advertisements as 'the world's largest collection of single-seater racing cars'.

This Donington International Collection, as it is called, is open all the year round but it is not the only local museum. You can watch the activities of the airport from the aeropark, a 12 acre area next to the taxiway, with various redundant aircraft on show and a visitor centre where Spitfire and other engines are on show together with cut-away models etc. This again, is open all the year round – except on Christmas Day. Before visiting the town take a look at Kings Mills, due west of the town and right on the county border, overlooking the river Trent. Mills were recorded here at the time of Domesday Book but now they have all gone and the place is, as one author has put it, 'in a setting of great beauty'. But close your eyes to the power station a mile further north!

And so to the town and the parish church which has the rare dedication to Edward, King and Martyr. 'Dunitone' in Domesday Book, the town added the prefix 'Castle', the site of which and much of the moat can still be seen north-east of the church. The castle was abandoned in 1564 and so, gradually, grateful local builders began to use this free quarry and many of the old stones may now be found built into some of the Castle Hill buildings. The town more or less encircles the church, and although there are not many houses of great interest, on the B6540 note the timber-framed Key House which carries the dates 1595 and 1636.

There is an extremely detailed history and guide to this large and interesting church – including the story of Edward, who was murdered in AD 978 so that Ethelred the Unready could become king. I will therefore just mention a few features. Note the unusual double squint in the Lady Chapel, the medieval memorial slabs inside the pulpit and the remains of a rood loft stairway in the north aisle. Even more interesting than the roof bosses in the nave, are the corbels; all but one are female heads. Finally, the handsome alabaster tomb of Robert Hasylryg and his wife Eleanor, and the brass ('one of the finest in the Midlands') of the 15th century depicting Robert de Staunton and his wife, should not be missed.

Leaving the town to the east in the direction of the M1 motorway and, subsequently, Kegworth, the minor road leads through *Hemington* where trenches of the Civil War still survive on slopes above the village and where the church has been in ruins for some 400 years. A short distance further on is *Lockington* where, in St Nicholas church above the chancel screen there is a huge coat of arms of Queen Anne dated 1704.

CHURCH LANGTON AND TUR LANGTON

———— There are actually five Leicestershire Langton villages of which Church Langton is the chief. It is the site of the mother church for the area, with an embattled tower which can be seen for miles. Tur Langton has the only post office and shop for all the five villages. The other Langtons are East, West and Thorpe Langton where the Baker's Arms (c1720) has a fine coat of arms sign.

St Peter's at *Church Langton* has a lofty tower and is notable for the incumbency of William Hanbury who will always be remembered as the man who, as Canon John Prophet, one-time vicar of Church Langton writes, gave the common folk of England their first taste of Handel's incomparable master-piece *Messiah*. In 1759 he organized a music festival and this was the first time that the oratorio was played in a parish church. In the church there is a piscina and a three-seat sedilia, all ogee-headed, and there is a crudely carved naked figure in the vestry passage near the 18th century organ. Above the pulpit is an opening – probably the remains of a rood loft – and two nearly identical tomb recesses can be seen in the outer walls of the south and north aisles.

Note also the date of the font – 1662 – which could make it one of the first to be installed after the Restoration, and a reredos in stone depicting the Last Supper. South of the church is the outsize rectory built by Hanbury's son, another William; a handsome symmetrical brick building which Pevsner praises as a house that 'would have been a credit to any affluent nobleman up the river Thames'.

A mile to the north is *Tur Langton*. Like Church Langton it stands astride the B6047 but with its village street straggling westward, and here the brick church of St Andrew, designed in 1866 by Joseph Goddard (mentioned previously for his restoration work) seems utterly out of place in a country village. It has the look of many Victorian churches in the middle of numerous towns which grew during the 19th century.

Near the end of this street the post office has the date '1728' over the entrance. The street veers right just past here and becomes the road to Kibworth Harcourt, but straight ahead is the wide drive up to the 17th century manor house. In a field beside it is an arch and other stones, the rather untidy remains of the old church which was demolished when building started on the new one. The owner of the manor house told me that the site was going to be more carefully preserved.

CLAYBROOKE MAGNA, CLAYBROOKE PARVA, HIGH CROSS, WIGSTON PARVA AND ASTON FLAMVILLE

—— Although there is barely an open stretch of land – and the school of 1837 – between them, there are two villages here albeit with only one church which is in *Claybrooke Parva*. On the other side of the B577 to the church is Claybrooke Hall which was considered 'modern' in 1846. Alongside the church is the Old Rectory – no longer used by the clergy but where the church key is kept.

In St Peter's church there is a guide available but I will add a few comments to the information given by the Rev. Stephen Haddelsey. The guide does not do justice to the chancel of c1340 which Arthur Mee says 'can bear comparison with that of any small church in the land'. This is mainly due to the six windows with identical flowing tracery. There are the remains of the rood screen and a newel staircase entrance leading to the sealed off door of the rood loft; the lectern is made of old bench ends. Do not miss the vicar's seat in the choir which recalls the VC won in the First World War by the Rev. A.H. Proctor who was vicar here between 1951 and 1963. Finally, note the great gallery of heads and figures, saintly and grotesque, in the nave roof and six stone faces on the arches below.

In *Claybrooke Magna*, a substantial brick farmhouse of the 18th century with a chequer-pattern façade faces the main road, but the most noticeable feature is directly opposite: an old chapel with one side removed and opened up as a workshop. Nearby is the 1897 village hall, and in Back Lane a 16th century timber-framed house.

A mile or so due west of Claybrooke Magna, the B577 terminates at the A5. Here also is where the A5 or Watling Street is crossed by another Roman road, Fosse Way, on its way to Ratae or Leicester. A monument shown on the Ordnance map as High Cross, stands here; erected in 1712 it is now in a poor state of repair. A barely decipherable plaque in Latin records the crossing of the two ancient roads and that this was the site of the small Roman settlement of Venonae.

After about a mile's drive up Watling Street, a turning to the right brings you to the tiny hamlet of *Wigston Parva* around a green where the map shows that it has a church without tower or spire. Actually the little church of St Mary, with nave and chancel all in one, has an open timber bell-turret and can boast a Norman north doorway. Hall Farmhouse dated 1727 faces the green along with the former manor house which is probably of an earlier date.

Though not actually connected with any of these villages or to High Cross, it is convenient to add *Aston Flamville*, some three miles to the north-west, a place which once was noted for its cheese. The present manor house is of the 18th century but the main reason for visiting this very small village is the dovecote in the field across the road. This was built in 1715, just three years after the High Cross monument. There is a silver jubilee badge on it and a plaque which reads: 'This building was restored in 1977 by the Powner Family of Aston Flamville in co-operation with the Blaby District Council'.

COSSINGTON AND ROTHLEY

These two villages are separated by gravel pits, the river Soar and the A6 trunk road, as well as by the original route of the A6, but I am indebted to *Who's buried where in Leicestershire* for being able to link them together. The father of Lord Kitchener, whose face and pointing finger adorned the recruiting posters in the First World War, came to live, and die, in Cossington. When staying with his father, Lord Kitchener would visit his sister who lived at Rothley Temple – now the Rothley Court Hotel. Now, having made the link, let us take each place in turn.

Cossington has a pleasant and prosperous look about it, with a number of attractive period buildings – several cruck cottages amongst them – along the B5328 which runs right through it. In the centre is the Royal Oak, recently re-opened after a disastrous fire, and not quite opposite is Christmas Cottage. Next door is the Manor House which was built in 1938 on the site of the old one, the home of Lord Kitchener's father. A few hundred yards further north is All Saints church and, just before the road bends away, is the black and white Magpie Cottage dated 1564. Immediately to the south of the church is the old rectory, now privately owned, which partly dates back to the 16th century, and which Pevsner calls 'One of the best small buildings in the county'. As you approach the church, you have a fine view of this gem and particularly of the large bay-window 'said to have come from a monastic house'.

Arriving at the church, first note, between the rectory and the churchyard, the elaborate arch-like doorway used by the incumbent in former times. Above the entrance is a panel within which is a coat of arms and the words 'Foy est Tout' and 'Erected April 1835'. Then, in the churchyard immediately outside the east window of the church, is the simple 1894

Lock between Cossington and Rothley on the river Soar.

grave of Lord Kitchener's father. Inside, first note at the east end of the north aisle the effigy of a priest in his Mass vestments of c1320. There is a good deal remaining of a stairway – presumably leading to a rood loft before the Reformation – but the greatest interest is in the chancel. A very lavish triple sedilia plus a piscina faces a tomb recess which is partly in the sanctuary, and two c1500 benches with linenfold panelling are against the screen. Finally note the coat of arms over the tower arch.

Leaving Cossington for Rothley, you pass a landscaped gravel pit – a haven for birds and a centre for leisure activities. As you cross over the river Soar, on the right there is Osier Villa dated 1875 but, on the left there is a lock (because of a weir) and the old Water Mill, now a popular restaurant. Drive straight on under the A6 trunk road, cross the old road and you arrive at the centre of *Rothley*. The present centre is Cross Green but the original one was Town Green and here are a number of cruck cottages, some with the woodwork clearly exposed. There is a 1779 house near the lychgate off Fowke Street into the church-yard of the unusually double dedicated church of St Mary the Virgin and St John the Baptist, and also period cottages in the short street opposite the ogee-headed doorway in the west tower.

Before looking at the church note the Rothley Cross a few yards from the south aisle, a Saxon cross some nine feet high and estimated to be of the mid 9th century. The tower has the familiar quatrefoiled lozenge frieze below the battlements, and it can be seen that the nave and the aisles are also embattled. There is a Norman font and a 15th century screen but the tombs – many of them containing members of the Babington family – must be our chief interest. Note particu-larly the inscription concerning the death of 'Anne, wife of Matthew Babington, of Temple Rothley, Esq...' She had '12 single births before the eldest was 12 years and 3 quarters old' with the last being still-born which 'proved also fatal to her mother'!

Temple Rothley, or Rothley Temple, got its name from the time the land belonged to the Knights Templar Order and their chapel of the mid 13th century is still there. I under-stand that a service is held once a year to keep it sanctified but when I looked in, all I saw was a rather dusty emptiness! When the Order was dissolved at the Reformation the Babingtons held the ownership of the estate – see above – and there are several memorials to record that this was the birthplace of the most celebrated of them all, Lord Thomas Babington Macaulay, the poet and historian, in 1800. He is not, however, buried locally: his last resting place is Westminster Abbey. The chapel is medieval but even parts of what is now the hotel can be dated back to that time although much of it is of the 17th or 18th century. Along the road to the station, through which steam trains run on the Great Central line between Loughborough and Leicester

North (see also *Quorn*), the boundary wall has a turret at each end which help to preserve the medieval image.

CROXTON KERRIAL AND BRANSTON

Saltby is virtually in a straight line north-west from Sproxton, and *Croxton Kerrial* is again almost on that same straight line in the same direction, with St John the Baptist church towering over the compact village on the north side of the A607 Melton to Grantham road. On the way in from Saltby there is the merest stump of a windmill, the last remains of four recorded over the years in the area. An unusual feature is the running water pump – part of an old water scheme – which stands just to the west along the Melton road; it has never been known to fail! Returning to the church via Middle Street, note No 21 with its arch and tower.

The mainly 15th century church has a central tower with eight pinnacles. The chancel is of ironstone but the rest of the church is in grey oolite. Part of a Saxon cross, dug up in the churchyard in 1968, is preserved at the east end of the south aisle between the tower arches, but the chief glory here, untouched by Gilbert Scott's restoration work in 1866, is the largest collection of pre-Reformation benches in the county; they are said to have come from Croxton Abbey at the time of the Dissolution c1540. The 42 benches have very ornate carvings on the poppyhead ends, including birds, dragons, a hunter with dogs, a man with two tongues etc, also various symbols and heraldic devices. Note also the many corbels with grotesque faces, not only in the nave but also in the chancel and in both aisles.

A few remains of the abbey walls and some of the fishponds, are in Croxton Park owned by the Duke of Rutland but, as the park is not generally open to the public, drive past the entrance on the A607 and take the first turning to the right for the little village of *Branston* whose rector also serves Croxton Kerrial together with the four parishes of Harston, Knipton, Saltby and Sproxton. Branston is a mainly ironstone village with a number of thatched cottages still remaining and opposite the church is the 1843 school – now the village hall.

The church is dedicated to St Guthlac, more or less a local Saint, for Guthlac was born and bred in the Midlands in the 7th century AD. As the church guide gives details of his life and the features in the church I will only draw attention to particular points not stressed in the guide, in particular the 1794 organ, originally in a Manchester church, which is situated in the west gallery. The coat of arms of George III and the Ten Commandments on wooden panels are above the chancel arch. Outside again, the tower is typical of the county – battlements, pinnacles and gargoyles but no frieze, and it is surmounted by a crocketed spire.

DADLINGTON, HIGHAM-ON-THE-HILL AND STOKE GOLDING

The village of *Dadlington*, just outside Stoke Golding, lies immediately south of the Bosworth Battlefield. The little 13th century church of St James – with nave and chancel all in one – has a notice board outside which reads:

'This church dates from the early 12th century. In 1511 Henry VIII founded a chantry here for the souls of those killed at the Battle of Bosworth fought at Redemore in this parish. The bodies of many of the slain were brought here to be buried.'

The church is situated at the entrance to the village green just opposite the curiously named Dog and Hedgehog inn. On the corner of the approach to the village from Sutton Cheney is Hall Farm, a large building which appears to be of the 18th century.

Stoke Golding, as a village, has little of hidden interest to offer, but history tells us that here is one more link with Bosworth Field. St Margaret's church has been called 'one of the most beautiful churches in Leicestershire' by Pevsner, and the late John Betjeman has written 'this is a church worth cycling twelve miles against the wind to visit!' It has a two-naved appearance because the south aisle and a chapel of c1280–90 were added as wide and as high as the nave. The capitals – some with foliage and some with heads – on the south arcade columns are the glory here. Pevsner says that 'the arcade was treated with a lavishness worthy of a cathedral', but read all about it in the church guide.

Outside, note the scratch dial in the middle of the wall near to the south door and that the tower has a parapet with a tracery frieze decoration under it. North of the church and at the bottom of the hill on the approach from Dadlington is the Zion chapel of 1853.

The present spire of St Margaret's church – itself only 'new' after an earthquake in 1580 wrecked the earlier one – was dismantled and stored during the Second World War because it was a hazard to aircraft landing at Lindley aerodrome. This aerodrome – between Higham-on-the-Hill and Fenny Drayton – is now a proving ground for the Motor Industry Research Association and can be clearly seen from the elevated grandstand of the churchyard of *Higham-on-the-Hill* where St Peter's has an early Norman tower. This is the main interest here, Norman towers being rare in the county – but otherwise there is much Victorian restoration. On Main Street the Methodist chapel is of brick and blue-black brick edging, and nearby is an old brick building opposite No 65, The Old Pump Cottage.

DESFORD, PECKLETON AND NEWBOLD VERDON

—— During the Second World War, trainee pilots flew from an airfield in the parish and there was the *Desford* mine. The site of the airfield is now occupied by a large factory, and the mine is no more, though part of the Desford pit winding wheel acts as a memorial outside the Miners Institute. Much of this large village comprises a housing estate but in the old part, in the High Street, is Old Manor Farm, with its two-storey porch, of c1630–40. Attached is a timber-framed barn and an 18th century dovecote can be seen through the gateway. A tourist attraction in the area is the Tropical Bird Garden in Lindridge Lane, marked on the Ordnance map.

As well as Old Manor Farm, there are a number of ageing buildings such as the Old Forge at the beginning of the Kirkby Road, and even some thatched cottages but the oldest building is St Martin's church. For visitors to this ancient church two members of the local history group have produced one of the most interesting and thorough guides that I have met in my researches. It is a little more expensive than most, but is complete with a glossary of architectural terms, so I need only mention two somewhat unusual features. An Easter Sepulchre – and few remain after Victorian restoration – is opposite the triple sedilia, and above the sedilia is a memorial in the shape of a book to commemorate the lives of Edward Muxloe and his wife Elizabeth who died in 1723, four years before her husband.

In the same parish is the tiny hamlet of *Peckleton* with the houses lying along the Kirkby Mallory road: amongst them is the 1877 school which was closed in 1961 and is now the village hall. The church is situated quite a step away from the village and is next to the hall; and the Peckleton Music Festival has become an annual event with the object of raising funds for the upkeep of St Mary Magdalene. This mainly early 14th century church has an even earlier piscina with dogtooth decoration next to a triple sedilia and opposite, under an ogee and cusped recess, are 14th century effigies of a cross-legged knight and his wife. Also in the chancel, but on the south wall, is another effigy of the same period – this time of a civilian. Preserved in a chancel window are some original glass fragments of the 14th century depicting a nun and St Michael, whereas the east window is by Kempe in 1894. Also in the south aisle is the front of a 16th century alabaster tomb-chest and, finally, note the hatchment over the tower arch.

At present it appears that the people of Desford have to go to *Newbold Verdon* to see a doctor, hence its inclusion in this section. Largely made up of housing estates, the interest lies in Main Street, with its old houses – including Cob Cottage built in 1650 – culminating with St James's church and, closing the cul-de-sac, Hall Farm which was rebuilt c1700 on a moated site. The church was virtually rebuilt in 1899, but note the squat pyramid-shaped spire of 1960. Returning to the centre where there are some shops, note the Baptist church of 1831 and the Primitive Methodist chapel of 1894 almost opposite each other. Just near the shops, standing out from amongst all the modern housing, is No 92, a cruck cottage.

DISEWORTH AND LONG WHATTON

These two villages, strung out along the B5401, are separated by the M1 and the A42 trunk road. Though they probably have little in common it is convenient to deal with them together. They are somewhat tenuously linked by the Long Whatton brook which flows between them and perhaps I will be forgiven for repeating the scandalous rumour in the WI Village Book. There used to be three brickyards in Diseworth with much of Loughborough said to have been built with bricks from these yards, 'local rumour has it that many of the houses in Long Whatton were built with bricks that fell from the carts going to Loughborough!'

Diseworth's four 'Gates' (or 'Streets') meet at what is locally called The Cross, and St Michael's church is situated at the Cross end of Hall Gate. A very complete history and detailed guide of the parish church is on sale inside so there is no need to go into great detail here. More helpful still, this guide also contains a brief history of both the Methodist church, built in 1887 at the other end of Hall Gate, and the Baptist church, in Lady Gate, which dates back to 1752. Just a few notes may be helpful.

You enter the parish church by the north porch. This is dated 1661 so perhaps it was added to celebrate the Restoration of Charles II. But inside, the coat of arms over the north door is not that of Charles II but of George II. The pulpit is dated 1713 and the bosses of the roof were restored in 1949; indeed, there is a plaque (made from the old roof timber) on the wall testifying that 'The roof of the nave was restored with English oak by craftsmen of this village 1949'. Langley Priory – now a proper house of the 17th and 18th century but originally a priory founded in 1154 for Benedictine nuns – lies some 1½ miles south-west of the village and here John Shakespear died in 1858. The Shakespear family, who were great benefactors to the church, had bought the priory from the Cheslyns, and there are tablets to both John Shakespear and the last of the Cheslyns in the chancel of the church. Arthur Mee tells us that this Shakespear, being inspired by the thought that he might be a descendant of the great Bard (with an 'e'), donated £2,500 towards preserving the poet's house at Stratford-upon-Avon.

Very near the Cross and west of the church, and nearly behind the little sub post-office, is a timber-framed and thatched cottage of the 16th century where one William Lilly was born in 1602. He became a very plausible astrologer, so much so that Cromwell granted him a pension of £100! He died in 1681 and is buried at Walton-on-Thames – a long way from home.

So, back eastwards along the B5401 to *Long Whatton* which apparently acquired the prefix 'Long' sometime in the 15th century because of its very obvious length. There is much vernacular building along the mile or so single street of the village but note particularly the timber-framed Keeper's Lodge (No 61) and the 17th century gabled cottages Nos 26 and 24. There is another old thatched cottage on the corner of a lane which leads to Whatton House, now the home of the Crawshaw family, which has lent its patronage to All Saints church.

The church stands on the other corner of the lane, with its lychgate opposite the thatched cottage, and the first thing you will notice is that the Norman tower forms the east end of the south aisle. This is unique in the county and as the very detailed guidebook says it 'hints in Long Whatton of a foundation much older than the standing fabric'. To supplement the guidebook I will only mention a few salient features. The drum-shaped font is Norman, the pulpit is Jacobean (circa 1613) but it has only been in All Saints since

1897 when it was brought from Great Shefford in Berkshire. Similarly, the fine late medieval screen was brought in 1894 from a ruined church at Colston Bassett in Nottinghamshire. Details of the glass and memorials are all given in the guidebook, and it closes with a reminder that we should look at the Swithland slate gravestones in the churchyard as we leave.

EAST NORTON AND TUGBY

Until the beginning of the 1990s the A47 trunk road passed right through East Norton and swept just north of most of Tugby; now, East Norton is bypassed and so, with less than two miles between them, I have united these two villages as a matter of convenience, hoping that the two places are not deadly rivals!

East Norton, already bereft of its railway by the axe of Dr Beeching, and now with the previously heavy road traffic no longer passing through, is a very quiet place; you have time to linger – and park! If you approach from the main road, there is only one turning off it at the west end of the village, and with the east end now blocked off the only other exit is by the unclassified road to Loddington. Starting from the east end, you will notice immediately the little sub post-office because of its bay-window and other mullion windows: the date '1643' is carved on the wall. Opposite is the police station and next door is a former inn still called the White Bull. Next door to that is a Georgian house called Smith's Cottage. It would have been virtually impossible, before the building of the bypass, to have studied these period buildings in this area of just a few hundred yards; now you can stand and stare from the middle of the road.

The ironstone All Saints church, which lies near to the main road turn off, is a small building and the most interesting features are the curiously shaped lintel over the doorway inside the south porch and the 14th century font. Of particular interest is a reredos containing carved figures etc behind the altar; this is dated 1928 'In memory of Mabel

Mary Heycock'. Note the board on the south wall recording the generosity of 'Richard Freestone, late of East Norton, Gent. gave ten pounds...for the poor of this parish and the interest to be paid on the 5th day of November forever'.

Now, having taken the A47 towards *Tugby*, the first building encountered when turning off the main road is the church of St Thomas à Becket, the key of which is obtainable at Chestnut Cottage nearby. There was much restoration in the 19th century but, fortunately, the four-storey tower was left untouched. The lower part is Saxon which, together with a little window, is a rare survival, and the top two storeys are post-Conquest. Inside, note the 13th century dog-tooth decoration over the priest's door and the eight angel corbels. On the north wall there is a beautiful monument to Richard Neeld dated 1574, and in the chancel another monument is to Thomas Wilson who died in 1699.

The village green is a short distance from the church and the old village pump stands opposite the Black Horse inn.

EASTWELL, EATON, GOADBY MARWOOD AND STATHERN

—— These four villages are not all that close together but, as three are part of the Scalford group parish and with all but Eastwell lying on the 15½ mile Jubilee Way footpath (between Melton Mowbray and Woolsthorpe-by-Belvoir, just over the border in Lincolnshire), it is convenient to deal with them together.

The church is the first building seen on approaching *Eastwell* from Scalford but, right next to it and alongside the road, are the 18th century stables, crowned by a cupola, of the 17th century hall. In Stanleys Lane, opposite the stables, is the former Roman Catholic chapel built in 1798 in lieu of one formerly in the hall; note the cross on the gable end. St Michael's church is most unusual and, to quote Hoskins, is 'utterly delightful both outside and in' with 'one of the most appealing country interiors...in the East Midlands'.

These two comments are repeated in the little guide, the availability of which means that, brief as it is, I need only add a few comments. The main feature is that the chancel is separated from the nave by a stone screen, like a wall, topped by a plaster tympanum above right up to the ceiling – an arrangement apparently found in only five other churches. The chancel is only visible through a narrow doorway flanked by two windows. On the tympanum is a hatchment of the Eyre family who owned the hall in the 17th and 18th centuries; in the chancel there is a 14th century effigy of a bareheaded priest. Note the iron lectern which was a gift to the church about 1860; when I visited it was tucked away at the west end of the south aisle!

Eaton is another small village but has its Main Street and Chapel Lane where the Methodist church is, and the 'Framland Church Trail' leaflet tells us that Thomas Wright, the third editor of Old Moore's Almanac once lived in a cottage in Main Street and that his gravestone can be seen in the churchyard. The church of St Denys is the highest point in the village and overlooks the Castle Inn nearby with its castle sign and a dummy knight, in full armour, standing atop an embattled section! The church is entirely built of ironstone including the unusual short spire. The tower has the local battlements, pinnacles and gargoyles but here there is no frieze. Note the mutilated piscina in the north aisle and, above it, an opening where the entrance to the rood loft used to be. In the north aisle there are corbels with grotesque faces, as there are on both sides of the nave roof, but only plain corbels in the south aisle.

The church at *Goadby Marwood* is also dedicated to St Denys, and appears very large and dominating, along with the hall, for what is now a very tiny and scattered hamlet. In Towns Lane there is a small Methodist church, which previously was a house and, where the road dwindles into a track, there is an old school which was about to be converted into the village hall. And so to the church where, apart from the building itself, the most interesting features are the four complete benches of c1500 – two in the chancel and two in the south aisle. Also in the south aisle is a tomb recess and, against the east end wall, a collection of coins and Roman bits and pieces presented to the church in 1991; these, no doubt, came from the Roman settlement unearthed during ironstone mining in the early 1950s. There are remains of rood loft stairs, an octagonal early 14th century font and ten corbels with grotesque faces holding up the nave roof.

Stathern is not exactly on the Jubilee Way but certainly veers towards it, and that is my excuse for its appearance here. First of all, at the north-west end, note the ironstone barn which has been converted into a house. In the middle of the village and opposite an Edward VII wall letterbox, is Chapel Lane with Chantry House and the Methodist church. Down a very narrow Church Lane is St Guthlac's which has a very comprehensive guide, not only for a visit to the church but it also contains a little Stathern history. Unlike many, this guide draws attention to the gargoyles, there are eight on the tower, and also to the carved heads on the corbels in the nave. Also, inside, note the ogee-headed piscina and a preserved bier. After leaving by the north doorway, go and look at the dogtooth decoration around the south doorway which is no longer in use.

FENNY DRAYTON

—— Originally called 'Drayton-in-the-Clay', Fenny Drayton is famed as the birthplace in 1624 of George Fox, the founder of the Society of Friends or the Quakers. The house in which he was born was demolished long ago but a memorial column stands on the corner of George Fox Lane and Old Forge Road. It is in the grounds of Monument House and difficult to see if driving past so you must park and walk back!

Dick Turpin, the famous highwayman, is reputed to have lived in the parish in the 1730s and a horseshoe – believed to be one from his equally famous horse – once hung in the smithy. This now belongs to the son of the last blacksmith who has restored the old forge with its cottage which can be seen opposite the end of Church Lane. Down the lane is St

Michael and All Angels church where you will find a helpful guide, not only to the church but also a little about the village and, of course, George Fox, so I need only add a few comments.

In particular, I would draw attention to the impressive six-post canopy tomb in the north aisle of George Purefoy, who died in 1628. The Purefoy family first came to Fenny Drayton in 1398 and William Purefoy signed the death warrant of King Charles I. Not mentioned in the guide are a late Norman doorway preserved in the south aisle, the remains of 18th century pews against the south wall, and pieces of c1600 panelling incorporated into the choir stalls. There is no clerestory but note a window over the chancel arch.

FOXTON AND GUMLEY

—— Foxton and Gumley are linked by the Grand Union Canal and, now a well-known tourist attraction, by what is called the Foxton Staircase: a series of ten locks which enabled barges in the heyday of the canal to climb the hill between the two villages. This remarkable engineering feat was completed in 1808 and the canal was a great commercial success. Now, however, commercial traffic is long gone although the canal is still in use for pleasure boats. Books about the locks and the canal can be obtained from the Bottom Lock shop so I need say no more.

In Main Street in *Foxton* village, the Baptist chapel of 1865 is built of local bricks, and nearby is the Old Court House overlooking the village. Set back from the road is the Shoulder of Mutton inn, and then, after crossing the canal and passing the Black Horse, you arrive at St Andrew's church. By the blocked up south doorway there is part of a Saxon cross, preserved in the church, but basically the church is of the 13th century with much, as is so often the case, 19th century restoration. The font has been dated to the middle of the 12th century, so it and the Saxon cross both pre-date the present building. As there is a good guide book here I will just summarise the features to look for: stairs leading up to where the rood screen used to be, an old clock of c1680, the blocked up leper's window in the chancel and the double aumbrey which is virtually behind the organ on the north wall.

Foxton is mentioned in Domesday Book but *Gumley* has a much older history. Records show that, in the year AD 749, the Mercian King Ethelbald held a witan or council here at 'Godmundeslaech' as it was called then, and that there was a Saxon palace of which nothing now survives. Gumley Hall, situated near the church, was demolished in 1962. Still surviving are the stables, originally attached to the demolished hall, near to the gate leading to St Helen's church. The stable tower is a splendid Italian campanile-style bell tower with a clock which apparently keeps perfect time. From here it is a short walk to the church where, once again, there is a little pamphlet with useful information. Not mentioned in it is a coat of arms over the disused north doorway, a little piscina in the south aisle and an elaborate memorial to John Norton and his wife (1705) on the west wall at the end of the south aisle.

FRISBY-ON-THE-WREAKE AND KIRBY BELLARS

The river Wreake is no longer navigable and the trains do not stop on their way between Melton Mowbray and Leicester, but this ancient village, instead of declining has actually increased in size. The name *Frisby*, listed as 'Frisebi' in Domesday Book, came about because the original settlers, the Frisians, came from the coast lands of North Holland or Germany but the modern settlers tend to commute daily into nearby towns!

In the village there are several cottages of the 18th century which are dated or otherwise embellished. I noticed this little plaque over the door of one cottage in the Main Street: 'Plenty of Grace be to this Place'. Around the corner from the Bell Inn is Georgian Cottage dated 1767 and on the corner of Church Lane with the alley leading up to the church is a house with a plaque bearing the initials S. J. C., dated 1796.

On the other side of this alley is the old school, dated 1854, with a plaque built into the wall stating 'Feed my Lambs'. Further along Church Lane is the vicarage, dated 1759.

Across the road from the Bell Inn is the old village cross and immediately south of the village, on the A607, there is a smaller cross shown as Stump Cross on the map. The Wesleyan chapel is dated 1863, and so to St Thomas of Canterbury church which can trace its ancestry back to a very much earlier century. The ironstone tower has a Norman lower stage but the top part, with pinnacles, gargoyles and quatrefoil lozenges under the battlements like so many locally, is of the early 14th century as is much of the rest of the church. There is a large arch on the chancel north wall with two corbel heads, and four small grotesque heads in the nave.

Just to the east of Frisby and immediately south of Asfordby is the hamlet of *Kirby Bellars* with the large St Peter's church, apparently out of all proportion to the present population and somewhat isolated; the original village disappeared centuries ago and the Ordnance map shows earthworks and the site of an old priory which can be seen just north of the church. The church has a four page guide, but there are a few other features to look out for which are not mentioned in it so get the key from Church Cottage between the church and the railway bridge then investigate.

In the churchyard are the remains of an old cross near the south porch. On entering the church, note the original iron hinges on the door. The 15th century chancel screen is mentioned but not the double sedilia and piscina in the chancel, and you will see five embossed corbels on both the north and south walls.

GADDESBY

——— 'One of the most striking and beautiful medieval churches in the Midlands, certainly among villages' (Hoskins) and 'One of the largest and most beautiful of the village churches of Leicestershire' (Pevsner) are two of the compliments heaped on St Luke's church at *Gaddesby*, so more than just a quick glance is needed to justify these remarks and an information sheet is available. First the exterior; note particularly the west end of the south aisle which has the look of a chantry chapel. The rich carving on the west wall is unusually lavish and dated c1323–1333. There are pinnacles all round this part of the south aisle, large gargoyles, three empty niches and it is embattled, unlike the rest of the south side of the church or the tower.

Inside the church has the appearance of being unrestored because there are so many medieval bench ends even where the seating has been renewed. There are also stone benches in the north aisle and around two pillars in the south arcade which, in medieval times, were for the aged and infirm. The screen, altar furnishings and reredos in the chancel are all Victorian but the piscina is 15th century. There are also piscinas in both the south aisle and the north aisle, where there is an altar tomb with an effigy of an unknown knight of circa 1500. Back in the chancel is a most unusual statue; an almost life-size sculptured monument to Colonel Cheney astride a dying horse. He was reputed to have had four horses shot from under him at the battle of Waterloo. The monument was sculptured by Joseph Gott in 1848 and previously housed in Gaddesby Hall until 1917. The then owner more or less arranged for the statue to be 'dumped' at the door of the church and then departed! A controversial siting perhaps, but there are very few statues of horses in churches!

The village has an opulent, very tidy, look, especially in the lane up to the church. Of the thatched cottages Cedar Cottage is of interest: the WI book tells us that the cedars here are descendants of some brought back by the crusaders. In Chapel Lane there are still two old pumps, and the older houses were at one time inhabited by workers at the Hall. Note that the inn is The Cheney Arms, named after the family of the gallant colonel mentioned earlier. Finally, as you leave Gaddesby for Ashby Folville along the B674, note the old windmill in a farm on the left-hand side of the road. Physically, perhaps, nearer to Ashby but as the WI book mentions it in their Gaddesby entry I will not argue.

GAULBY AND KINGS NORTON

—— Arthur Mee, in 1937, has just one entry headed 'Norton-By-Gaulby' in which he writes only about Kings Norton and ignores Gaulby altogether. Today, these two hamlets have distinctly separate entities and they are linked here only because of their unusual churches. They can be seen one from the other, were built or rebuilt by John Wing or his son, another John, for the local squire, William Fortrey, in the middle of the 18th century.

If you approach *Gaulby* from Billesdon, you pass the site of the deserted village of Frisby, and then the odd pagoda-like pinnacles of St Peter's church hold your attention as they come into view. First, however, note the Edward VII letter box on the wall across the road from the church, and the 1932 sundial above it. Of the original church the pre-Reformation chancel remains but the tower and much of the nave was rebuilt in 1741 by John Wing. The tower has the date on the south side and you certainly will not see such 'craziest' (Pevsner) pinnacles elsewhere!

Unseen now, but under the carpet in the chancel is the oldest memorial in the church, to Martha Tookey who died in 1612. At the west end are slate slabs on the floor to the memory of Robert Foster, Gent and his wife, and to John Dand, Gent and his wife. The memorial to John Dand's wife recalls that 'she lived in the honourable state of wedlock with her said husband fifty five years...she departed this life aged 83 years'. Considering the expectancy of life in the 18th century, this would appear to be an extraordinary age for the period. Note the font, also of 1741, which looks very much like an urn. There were box pews here until they were removed during some restoration work in 1960.

William Fortrey actually lived in *Kings Norton*, and appears to have been the squire of both communities. The manor house and a dovecote can be seen just to the east of the church of St John the Baptist. He commissioned the younger John Wing to rebuild the church; this work, except for the spire on top of the tower, was completed in 1761, 20 years after his father's work at Gaulby. According to Pevsner the result makes this building not only one of the most important in the county but 'one of the most remarkable in England'. The spire completed in 1775, was destroyed during a thunderstorm in 1850, never to be rebuilt because of the cost. A contemporary newspaper account of the catastrophe is framed on the wall near the entrance.

From the outside, St John's has the look of a small cathedral but the first surprise on entering is the absence of coloured glass, so making the aisleless building, with no structural division between the nave and the chancel, very light indeed unlike so many other churches. The three-decker pulpit, the box pews, and the complete retention of Fortrey's original design, are remarkable features which provide the justification for Pevsner's claim. The pulpit, the reading desk and clerk's desk are situated right in the centre of the east end of the nave, an extremely rare position today, acting as the boundary between nave and chancel. The original box pews in the nave are normal whereas the box pews in the chancel end (behind the pulpit) face each other as in a choir.

There is a gallery at the west end and underneath a christening pew round the 1850 font; this replaced the original 18th century font which was destroyed, as well as part of the fabric, when the spire fell in the thunderstorm. Note the coat of arms above the gallery. Outside, before leaving the church-yard have a look at the fine memorial which William Fortrey erected to his father and mother immediately east of the chancel. Then go out through the gate piers with the original iron gate and look left along the wall which runs along to the entrance to The Limes; there is a well set into the wall and on it is one of the plaques – several are mentioned elsewhere in this book – erected to commemorate the silver jubilee of Queen Elizabeth II. The little brick house by the gate is the original rectory, and I was shown by the present owner a large pre-1850 print of the church complete with its spire.

GREAT BOWDEN

This large village is the original settlement of Market Harborough, but whereas that settlement has developed into a sizeable town, Great Bowden still retains the traditional characteristics of a village with its series of greens and, despite the usual in-filling, picturesque cottages and a number of old houses. Approaching from the A6, you cross a narrow bridge over the Market Harborough arm of the Grand Union Canal, past Waterways Cottage and Great Bowden Hall and then, having crossed the railway line which runs between Kettering and Leicester, you arrive at the centre of the village.

The centre is grouped round a very pleasant large green, so that the points of interest are not so much hidden as acting like spokes from a wheel. On the east side, in Knights End Road, is a little white painted cottage with a plaque on it which reads 'JN * August the 12 1797'. On the other side of the green, the Old Forge is now a private house. A few hundred yards to the north is the church of St Peter and St Paul, the large rectory and the old National school dated 1839. The school, which is now the church hall, is of brick except for the side which abuts the churchyard and this is of ironstone. The rectory, which stands to the north-west of the church, is a typical 17th century example of seven bays and two storeys – impossible for the modern clergyman to maintain today.

As the church is one of those where there is a comprehensive, illustrated guide, I need not go into too much detail, so here are just a few highlights. The tower is embattled at the top with cross-slits, pinnacles, quite a short spire and a gargoyle in the middle of each side below the embattlements. Inside, this is another church where the remains of the stairway to a rood loft are at the south-east end of the nave, but the chief glory here is a painting of a Doom or Last Judgement which is in the north chapel, now used as the vestry. There is another wall painting on the south wall of the south chapel. These paintings were restored in 1961 by Dr E. Clive Rouse, the leading expert on wall paintings.

GREAT DALBY

——— From whatever direction you approach Great Dalby the first impression is the same – that of the traditional (perhaps only legendary) appearance of 'ye olde English village': a very open village green with a war memorial surrounded by cottages, even though many here are somewhat larger. It is, indeed, a very old village and the church guide implies that there was a Danish settlement here before the Norman Conquest. As always, there is in-filling but there are still thatched cottages and even some cruck buildings; the Wesleyan chapel is dated 1846. St Swithun's church (Pevsner has mistakenly entered this as St. Swithin's) is tucked away up a path from the green. Although fairly central it is less dominant than many churches because of the collapse of the spire in 1658.

St Swithun's Church, Great Dalby: A brief history is available in the church so I need not go into great detail. It gives you the whole sad story of the collapse together with an explanation of the present appearance of the rebuilt nave. Arthur Mee likens it to 'the hall of a Jacobean manor house...with mullioned windows reaching almost to the roof and old shields set between.' The guide mentions the coat of arms of George III over the chancel arch, and also that a modern reproduction hangs on the north wall of the nave. Note that the old parish chest, with its three locks, is thought to be of the 14th century and that the ironwork on the south door is medieval.

GREAT EASTON AND BRINGHURST

——— On arriving at Great Easton, my first impression was of the openness of the centre of the village with the village green in the middle on which stands the war memorial to those who fell in both World Wars. Around this green, and elsewhere, are several houses of different centuries but my second impression was that I could not see the church! It is, in fact, up a steep incline off the Horninghold Road at the north end of the village; it is normally open and well worth a visit.

I was fortunate to meet a local historian who told me a few facts about the church, and pointed out that a large tomb in the churchyard – standing a few feet from the south porch – had been designated a 'Listed building' but he could not tell me why! The church has a very comprehensive guide, so I will only mention a few of the more interesting items. Strangely, the guide does not mention the listed tomb.

Within the north wall of the chancel, under a very graceful 14th century arched recess with an ogee gable, is an alabaster effigy lying on a stone slab. There is no inscription and, according to *Memorials of Old Leicestershire* the effigy is certainly of earlier date than the recess. The carved panels of the pulpit are Jacobean and the guide suggests that it may well have been part of a three decker arrangement which was dismantled in 1832. The coat of arms, on the board above the door into the tower, is that of King William III and is a rare instance of William without Mary.

Outside again, and immediately after turning right out of the porch, note a mass or scratch dial, a primitive form of sun dial, on a buttress supporting the south west corner of the south aisle. Look up at the tower and note the corbel tables with carved stone faces at the top of all four sides of the tower just below the broach spire. Finally, note the herringbone pattern of stones on the west face of the north aisle. It is suggested that this is a fragment of a very early church – possibly one of pre-Conquest date.

The guide urges the visitor to 'look round St Nicholas, Bringhurst, the parent church of Great Easton'. So, leaving by the Medbourne road via some attractive thatched houses and the school on the hill, *Bringhurst* stands on a hill virtually overlooking Great Easton: although originally the parent church, it is tiny compared with its now much larger 'offspring' – both church and village. I was unable to enter the ironstone church but it has a good Norman north arcade. Note the gargoyles in the middle of the top of each side of the tower. Just south of the church is a house with a gable, and over the door is a lintel with the inscription 'Anno Domini 1636'.

THE GREAT STRETTON OR STRETTON MAGNA AREA

At the beginning of the 1990s the inhabitants of Great Glen, Burton Overy and Little Stretton, also Houghton-on-the-Hill, Gaulby and Kings Norton (dealt with elsewhere) were much concerned about a major development plan to build a massive complex involving the present Leicester East aerodrome, hundreds of houses, office blocks and two golf courses etc, the whole to be known as 'Stretton Magna'. This name was apparently chosen because the now deserted village of Great Stretton was situated more or less centrally in the plan. Though the plan was abandoned, it does conveniently link these places together.

Great Glen is a village situated just off the A6 and some six miles from the big city but, having grown considerably since the Second World War, it has a 'towny' look about it at the centre. St Cuthbert's church was thoroughly restored in 1876 although a Norman doorway, with horses carved on its capitals, survives in the nave. In 1769 the tower was partly rebuilt by John Wing (see *Kings Norton*) but it escaped the 1876 restoration. There are also three Anglo-Saxon stone fragments preserved, the remnants of a pre-Conquest church. The Methodist church stands near the centre crossing with a stone inscribed 'Wesleyan Chapel 1827' and another recording the addition of '1879'. Most of the older buildings are along Main Street, among them 'The Old School House 1846' which is now a surgery. At the village green end of Main Street, before it joins the main road, there are several dated houses such as Bridge House of 1748 and, flanking the main road, both The Crown and The Greyhound inns have a long history.

Burton Overy, situated between Great Glen and the old Roman Road (now Gartree Road) running from Colchester to Leicester, lies in a valley. The church of St Andrew is on a slight eminence; I was unable to obtain entry but it has an early 14th century sedilia and piscina as well as an impressive 15th century screen. Outside, note the large gargoyle between the two east windows (of the chancel and the north chapel) and there is another large gargoyle near the south porch. The old rectory, immediately west of the church, is of brick and dated 1710. Almost across the road from the church is what has become a private house owned by an architect; it bears the legend 'Independent Chapel 1852' and there are still gravestones in the garden.

Little Stretton, at the point of a triangle with Great Glen and Burton Overy, is a tiny hamlet but the small ironstone church of St John the Baptist, which stands at the north end, has a Norman nave and, as Hoskins says, is very appealing. The manor house can be seen from the church, but only the church, which stands at the north end of the hamlet, concerns us here. There was some careful restoration in 1899 but basically it must look now as it has done since the chancel was rebuilt in circa 1300 – no aisles and no north facing windows. There are some 17th century pew heads but one poppyhead is much older than that. The octagonal font is of Purbeck marble and beside it is a bell, founded in 1781, which was removed from the little tower because of the weight.

Great Stretton now consists of St Giles church and one or two farm buildings. The outlines of the former village – now completely vanished – can be made out in aerial photographs with the bumps and hollows where houses stood, and a moated manor house is very clearly defined. I was unable to visit the church because the field in which it stood was protected by barbed wire, but it looked very forlorn.

GRIMSTON AND SAXELBYE

——— *Grimston* lies between the two main roads A606 and A6006. As you approach the village after turning off the B676 which links them, the first thing to strike you is that there are inns on either side of a green. The right hand one is called the Old Stocks and, sure enough, there on the green are the old village stocks. Just across from the stocks is a house with what looks like a school bell; indeed it had been the old village school and the bell retained on what is now a private dwelling. On the other side of the green is the Black Horse.

On the way to St John the Baptist church, you pass the brick built Wesleyan church. To visit the church, you must park in the road by the letter box and telephone kiosk (marked on the Ordnance map). You will see the old village pump on the other side of the road opposite a cottage called The Paddock. The church is open and as a comprehensive guide is available just a few additional words will suffice. Pinnacles and gargoyles with the quatrefoiled lozenge frieze below the battlemented tower are typical of many churches in the area, and in the churchyard are the base and the lower part of the shaft of a cross – completely covered in ivy on my visit. Inside, note the double piscina with pointed-trefoil arches in the south transept and the clock of circa 1600 which has been resited on the north wall.

I have bracketed the rather scattered village of *Saxelbye* with Grimston because they are very close and the Ordnance map shows the Saxelby (without an 'e') Pastures immediately east of the village of Grimston. There are a number of ironstone farms here and the mainly 13th century ironstone church of St Peter. This has the usual local frieze below the battlements of the tower with the addition of a crocketed spire (leafy knobs all the way up). Note the late 15th century octagonal font with castellations; a screen of the same period was dismantled during 1856 renovations and the panels were built into the pulpit. The south porch was also rebuilt at this time and the original piscina placed in it. The present piscina in the sanctuary is no doubt Victorian!

Beside the altar is a large incised slab depicting an armed man, supposedly one Robert Brokesby, dated 1531. Details in the church inform us that it came from *Shoby* and that it must have been brought to Saxelbye before 1600.

The remains of a monastic farm – originally connected with

Launde Abbey – are intermingled with Priory Farm (shown on the Ordnance map as 'Chapel') at Shoby some two miles along a minor road to the west, just before this meets the A6006.

HALLATON

Hallaton, situated more or less midway between the county boundary and the A47, is widely known for its centuries old custom of Bottle-kicking and Hare-pie Scrambling – a contest without rules between Hallaton and Medbourne on Easter Monday. The centre-piece of the village is a little green on which stands a conical market cross and it is here that beer from what is actually a small keg is drunk. There is a plaque here, one of several erected to celebrate the Silver Jubilee of Queen Elizabeth II in 1977 which sets out the full story of this traditional custom.

Just a few yards from the cross is the Bewicke Arms with a fine coat of arms for a sign. To the north of the cross, but somewhat overshadowed by a building, is a 17th century oblong conduit just across the road from the little sub-post office. Nearby is the Congregational chapel dated 1822 with a large clock. The west side of the village is dominated by St Michael's and All Angels church which Pevsner calls 'One of the most imposing of Leicestershire village churches'. As you walk towards it down Churchgate, note the old pump and well close by No 10. On the outside of the north wall of the chancel is a rococo obelisk to George Fenwicke, who died in 1760, and this almost faces the cottages which he endowed for 'three Antient Poor Women'.

Before entering the church by the north porch have a look at the Norman tympanum depicting St Michael slaying a dragon. Considered the finest in the county, this was previously over a former doorway and is now set into the side of the porch itself. Inside, there is a piscina and a three-stepped sedilia in the chancel – much dog-tooth carving here – and another ogee-headed sedilia in the south aisle. The pulpit, with its linenfold panels, is of the 18th century and

The conical market cross, Hallaton.

the Early English font is drum-shaped with carvings of heads and evil beings. Finally, note the corbel faces at the west end of the north aisle and, outside once again, the corbel tables on the tower below what Pevsner calls 'the best 13th century broach-spire in the county'.

In Hog Lane a small museum of local bygones is open at weekends during the summer months. Across the road from the duck pond there is a fairly modern almshouse with the inscription 'Isabella Stenning Charity Erected 1924'. Nearby are two old cottages, Ivy Cottage and Rose Cottage; opposite is the entrance to 18th century Hallaton Hall. Now called Torch House, it is occupied by the Torch Trust for the Blind where the reading of Braille and similar activities are taught.

HATHERN

—— Driving through outlying Loughborough to Kegworth on the A6 turn off at the little cross-roads into *Hathern*, first mentioned as 'Avederne' in Domesday Book, where there are several 'hidden' features.

In the centre of the village is the old village cross with its steps and part of the shaft preserved; nearby is a cruck-construction house. Down a lane from the cross is St Peter's and St Paul's church with a dated clock on the tower and across the road is St Aloysius Roman Catholic church. In St Peter's is what Pevsner calls a 'curious' window in the chancel; the top part is a single ogee-headed light and under-neath are two small lights side by side. To the right of the altar there is a gruesome memorial with a skull over an aumbry and a piscina opposite. The font is modern, but do not miss the ancient arcaded font of uncertain date though believed to be Anglo-Saxon, and the coat of arms over the tower door.

HOSE, HARBY, PLUNGAR, BARKESTONE-LE-VALE AND REDMILE

—— The Nottingham to Grantham canal, opened in 1793 and now disused, enters the county to the west of Hose, and flows placidly through the Vale of Belvoir more or less along the line of the county boundary (but certainly not parallel with it) around or near to all these five villages and then leaves the county just south of Muston. I hope that you will agree that I am justified in linking these villages in a single section.

The very compact village of *Hose* has a history reaching back at least to the time of Domesday Book when it was listed as 'Hoches' or 'Howes'. The name could have come from an earlier Old English name 'Hohas' meaning 'hills'. The 14th century St Michael's church is mostly of ironstone although the early 16th century clerestory is of limestone. As, unusually, the south porch is blocked up, the church is entered by the north. Note the seats or benches in the porch which are, according to the information available, probably parts of the medieval stone altar.

The font is octagonal, decorated on the bowl with angels with outstretched wings. There are ten small medieval bosses on the wall of the south aisle over where the south doorway used to be, and where the vestry now is. The most important relic here is on the base of the column supporting the north side of the chancel arch; traces of medieval red paint can clearly be seen. Outside again note that the pinnacles on the tower are square in shape – unlike those on so many of the county's churches.

A mile or so to the north-east is *Harby*, where, like Long Clawson and Scalford, there is an active Stilton creamery and where, in times past, their tower mill by the canal was rated as one of the finest in Britain. It is now but a stump, the canal wharf, as at Hose, has gone, but still standing is a granary, built in 1836. The WI book tells us that, whereas at one time ironstone was reserved for prestigious buildings, local brickyards supplied materials for many of the cottages, and Exchange Row is a terrace of brick cottages built by the Great Northern Railway. In Watsons Lane, leading off from the square in which the war memorial stands and opposite the pathway to St Mary's church, there are some interesting exteriors including ironstone The Yews and No 37, The Cross House. The war memorial has a fragment of an old village cross built into it, and nearby is the ironstone school of 1860 which is still in use: it has particularly attractive carvings and an ogee-headed doorway.

St Mary's is another ironstone church mostly early 14th century although the chancel arch is of the previous century with nailhead decoration. There is a George II coat of arms and here again the font is octagonal and contemporary with the building: the date 1606 was carved in later! In the nave there are five corbels on each side supporting the roof, each with a grotesque face.

Taking the road out of Harby towards Bottesford but, after about a mile, turning left just short of the disused railway bridge, you are then running roughly along the canal and on the way to the other three villages. St Helen's church in

Plungar, as a guide sheet says, is 'rich in animal symbolism' and there are two carved animals on the right-hand choir stall heads of c1500 brought from Croxton Abbey; the other choir stall animals are Victorian designed to harmonise with the medieval ones. The most precious relics here, however, are the three carved stone plaques – illustrating one of the many tales relating to Reynard the Fox – situated on the exterior of the west wall of the tower. They also are believed to come from Croxton Abbey and are dated c1450. Note the eight angels on the roof corbels, and that the 15th century font has a battlemented bowl.

Moving on to *Barkestone-le-Vale* you will see the stump of another windmill on the way to the church of St Peter and St Paul. Note the chimneys of Orchard Farm in Chapel Street. In the centre of the village is the old school dated 1819. The ironstone tower of the church has battlements and pinnacles whilst the south doorway retains Norman zigzag ornamentation, but much of the church was restored in 1840. There are four stall ends circa 1500, some unusual iron poppyheads, and a 14th century effigy of a lord of the manor in the north aisle.

At *Redmile*, where there used to be a private railway station for the Duke of Rutland in Belvoir Castle, the canal flows very near the north-west edge of the village. The Peacock Inn stands between it and St Peter's church with its crocketed spire. Further down the street is the school dated 1871 and the Primitive Methodist chapel of 1809, a cottage of 1838 and some other cottages which all have mouldings around the windows. In the church there are more c1500 benches with poppyheads and another octagonal font with flowers on its panels. Outside note the many gargoyles and, in the churchyard, the base and shaft of a cross.

HOUGHTON - ON - THE - HILL

—— Only six miles out of Leicester this large village appears to be more self-contained than many because it has garages (albeit on the A47), shops and a pharmacist in a converted forge, but it is still a village and of very ancient vintage. In Scotland Lane near the war memorial end there are several old cottages where the road narrows. Around the corner leading into Main Street are Granary Cottage and Bakehouse Cottage – the names giving the clue to their previous owners' occupations – and then the general store and what was the old forge.

The old village is mercifully south of the A47 and as you go down Main Street towards the church, you will see the Wesleyan chapel of 1852 – now the Methodist church – next to the large Hall Farm House opposite the Old Black Horse inn. Nearly at the end of Main Street and opposite the church is Church Farm which has a timber-framed wing at the back with a brick front added, apparently, in 1718, but with '1710' picked out in black bricks on the side wall! Next door is Eaton House which could be of the same period. Next to the church, the old rectory of 1856 is now in private hands, and the rector accommodated in a more economical house elsewhere in the village.

St Catherine's church is at one end of the village but this has a simple explanation; a teacher pointed out humps and folds in the fields behind the school where the original village stood in medieval times. Those villagers would have seen the church very much as it is today because it is basically all 14th century. No guide is available as I write but I was fortunately able to borrow an illustrated one, now out of print, from the rectory.

Two features are immediately apparent in the church. There is no clerestory but the two rectangular windows over the chancel arch, of the 14th century, were revealed during repair work in 1907; work in 1903 uncovered the remains of a piscina or a sedilia in the north aisle and the guide suggests that this could be dated between 1272 and 1307. There are corbels with carved heads in both aisles and the millstone shaped font is of the 13th century. The old stone seat under a window in the south aisle was for the use of the old and infirm in the days when there was no seating in churches, and the origin of the expression 'Let the weakest go to the wall'.

——— Although the villages of Baggrave, Cold Newton, Ingarsby, Lowesby and Quenby – all marked on the Ordnance map – were deserted or actively depopulated in the 14th or 15th centuries, the village of *Hungarton*, the largest of these settlements, managed to survive and, at one time, the parish embraced most of these places. In the church there is a monument in the Quenby chapel to Shukburgh Ashby who 'from a principle laudable and disinterested' largely rebuilt the village in the 1760s and 1770s and so, in the Main Street just below the church, there is a house of 1766 and opposite one of 1769. Nearby are the Old Forge and Vicary House dated 1772. The Black Boy is now the only inn in the village; the church key is kept at the former Ashby Arms, now a working farm immediately below the south front of the church.

St John the Baptist church is mainly of the 14th century with the usual alterations over the years but you can read all about it in the very comprehensive guide which also includes a brief look at local history. I have mentioned one Ashby memorial in the Quenby chapel; but a number of other Ashby memorials were put up in this chapel during their 400 years at Quenby Hall. Note particularly the clever design of that to George Ashbie who died in 1672: two sculpted angels are holding a curtain open for the inscription to be read. Quenby Hall, built about 1620 by George Ashbie, is considered to be the most important early 17th century house in the county and stands just over a mile from the village. Visitors are not encouraged.

Two miles to the north-west is *Beeby*, a tiny hamlet where All Saints church is looked after by the Churches Conservation Trust (formerly the Redundant Churches Fund). The church is usually open and being agreeably surprised as there is a guide on sale to help the funds, I need not go into great detail. The guide mentions the 14th century screen but there are also remains of stairs to the former rood loft. The stalls on the south side of the chancel might once have been misericords. You cannot fail to comment on what is known as the 'Beeby Tub' – the truncated spire, about which there are various legends as to why it is as it is!

Just north of the church is a curious structure which is a well with a stone cover, erected originally in 1855, and restored in 1953 to commemorate the coronation of Queen Elizabeth II. The inscription reads as follows:

In Summer's heat, and Winter's cold
One constant temperature I hold
When Brooks and Wells and Rivers Dry
I always Yield a good Supply,
My Neighbours say I'm Often Told
I'm more than worth my Weight in Gold.

HUSBANDS BOSWORTH AND THEDDINGWORTH

These two villages make a natural pair, being adjacent to each other along the A427 Lutterworth to Market Harborough Road, flanked (roughly) on the north by the Grand Union Canal and on the south by the river Welland running along the county boundary. In some old books *Husbands Bosworth* is shown with an apostrophe between the 'd' and the 's', and it is on record that, at some stage in its history, the first word of the name was added to distinguish it from Market Bosworth. It was the farmers' or husbandmen's Bosworth as opposed to the town people's or market people's Bosworth.

In Berridges Lane there is a Baptist chapel of 1807 and in the Welford Road the primary school of 1857 still operates. On the eastern edge of the village, just off the road, and built in 1873–74 is St Mary's Roman Catholic church, built in the grounds of the Hall by Sir Francis Turville who died in 1889 and remembered by his effigy. Probably the most interesting period houses are to be found in Honeypot Lane. A timber-framed house has the date 1712 picked out in blue brick, and opposite No 34 is early 19th century with what look like modern battlements over the side door.

All Saints church, situated just off the main road, has a

14th century tower and a south porch of 1746. This, with the remains of a double sundial on the top was completed not long before the old spire was struck by lightning in 1755. The present broach spire and octagonal pinnacles replaced the old structure some time after. Note the niche on the west wall of the tower and the row of faces just under its top.

And so eastwards, and even nearer to the Northampton-shire border, to *Theddingworth*. The original medieval settlement, shown in Domesday Book as 'Tedingesworde' or 'Tedigworde' was slightly to the north of the present village which is strung out along the main road. Although mainly of the late 13th to early 14th century, All Saints church in the centre of the village has a Norman north arcade of 1190–1200 so the church has stayed put despite the demographic movement over the centuries. Approaching the village from the west, virtually the first building is the Smeeton Institute – built by John Smeeton in memory of his son in 1893 – and this is now the village hall. Nearby is the red brick Gothic styled Congregational chapel of 1833. In Station Road (the railway is now dismantled) there are estate cottages dated 1851, and in the Sibbertoft Road are the six three-storeyed Pebble Cottages, built originally in 1829 for workers making silk plush for top hats.

In the church note the 1754 Snetzler organ; apparently this is one of only three in the country. The remains of a 15th century screen are built into the fronts of the nave benches but the nine foot high font cover is only of 1893. In the north chapel there is an elaborate and lofty monument with no inscription, but the arms at the top are reckoned to be those of George Chambre of Potten who died in 1635. This monument has effigies of a man and a woman – one above the other – and below are two sons and two daughters, all kneeling. On the south wall of the same chapel is a mural monument to George Bathurst who died in 1656 and his wife, who died six years earlier, with their 17 children!

Although now in Northamptonshire, Hothorpe Hall, in the park down Sibbertoft Road, used to be the residence of the lords of the manor of Theddingworth. It is now run as a Christian conference/holiday centre and community.

KEGWORTH

During a normal domestic flight between London and Ireland in January 1989, a British Midland aircraft was suddenly in trouble. Failing to reach the runway of East Midlands airport it crashed into the side of the M1 motorway, with the loss of 47 lives. The pilot was praised for saving Kegworth from another Lockerbie type disaster, which had happened only a few weeks earlier, and since then this terrible accident has been labelled by the media as the Kegworth Air Disaster. There is now a memorial plaque on the bridge over the motorway nearest to where the accident happened, and the villagers continue to live with the knowledge that it is only the motorway which separates them from the runway.

I write 'villagers' but it is difficult to decide whether the place is a large village or a small town. It is listed in the 1086 Domesday Book as 'Cogeworde' and in the 19th century was the centre of the knitting trade. It was certainly thought of then as a prosperous little town, especially as there was also an active canal trade. Today, the old framework knitters workshop may be seen preserved behind the Britannia Inn and the barges – you must call them 'narrow boats' – on the river Soar only carry passengers who want a leisurely holiday. Industry today is certainly here but of a different sort. A high-tech computer base for a well-known bank and a mineral water complex together with the airport ensure that employment is not a great problem. There are still hidden parts, in the main these are to be found close together in what would have been the original village and, of course, the lynchpin of that is St Andrew's church.

This large church, opposite the market place, is kept locked but they will tell you in the post office who has the key and then, once inside, you will be greatly impressed by the large coat of arms of King Charles II over the chancel arch. Erected in 1684, it is 20 years older than the very similar one of Queen Anne at nearby Lockington. As this is another church which has not only a good guide but also a *Transcript of a framed, handwritten history* I will just mention a unique feature; the vertical brackets helping to support the nave roof have been carved to represent medieval bandsmen. Although restored in 1954, the chancel roof still has the traditional angels on the corbels. Incidentally, due to the raising of the level of the nave in the 19th century there is now no step up into the chancel.

Just round a sharp bend and a few hundred yards from the market place on what is the London Road leading to Lough-borough, is the Great House: the date is shown over the doorway in its segmental pediment 'MDCXCVIII [1698]'. Behind the church is a timber-framed building – Harrison House and The Old School – which has the date '1575' over the door. In the High Street there is a local museum which contains items only from the village itself. The remaining thatched house in Kegworth is also here in the High Street.

KIBWORTH HARCOURT, KIBWORTH BEAUCHAMP AND SMEETON WESTERBY

The Ordnance Survey map shows a windmill situated just outside Kibworth Harcourt on the approach road from Tur Langton, and there is, indeed, a finely restored postmill, complete with its sails, on the left hand side but if you drive too fast you will miss it. It is in a farmyard behind a high hedge and, as it is the only postmill in the county, well worth stopping to investigate. The two Kibworths are bisected by the A6 trunk road, and after some modern suburban-type houses in the smaller *Kibworth Harcourt*, you come at once upon what is known locally as the Old House which, in 1678, was one of the first brick-built buildings in the county. Diagonally across the road, No 37 is another brick house of 1702; note the fire insurance mark high up on the wall facing the road.

On the A6 there is another house dated 1704 and next door is the Congregational church, dated 1756. *Kibworth Beauchamp* is on the south side of the A6. The first building you will see is the 14th century church of St Wilfrid, which acts as a link between the two villages and it is, in fact, the parish church of both. Despite the antiquity of the church note that the tower only dates from 1832; it was rebuilt after the spire collapsed.

Station Road, down from the church, crosses the railway and at the triangle, where it meets the High Street, there is the old parochial school of 1812; long disused as a school, it is now put to good use as the 'Old School Surgery'. Across from the triangle and opposite the Old Swan inn, No 4 High Street, Lantern House, has a giant blank arch framing the arched middle window. Westward along the High Street, turn right into School Road and you will find the buildings of the old 1725 grammar school which were, until recently still being used by Kibworth High School.

Practically opposite School Road, a minor road leads south to *Smeeton Westerby* – only about a mile from its larger neighbour but, I understand, jealous of its independence. In the main street of the village No 33 was the Old Forge and No 57 the Old Bakehouse, and the WI Village Book mentions an ironstone wall, saved from demolition by the villagers, which still retains the mullioned windows of a former house. The little Christ Church, built 1848–49, has an octagonal bell-turret and inside there is stained glass by Kempe in the south aisle window.

KIRBY MUXLOE

—— This village is fast becoming a suburb of Leicester and, as the c1300 St Bartholomew's church was largely restored in the middle of the 19th century, it might be thought that Kirby Muxloe had nothing of interest to offer, but there is one extremely important feature: the very picturesque ruin of the moated castle which is now in the charge of English Heritage.

It is really a castle in name only because in 1480 William, Lord Hastings, who also built the stone tower now bearing his name at Ashby-de-la-Zouch, was actually enlarging an already existing fortified manor house. Although there is a stone gateway, the building is brick built; the full details are

Doorway of gatehouse, the castle, Kirby Muxloe.

in the excellent English Heritage booklet. The work was never completed, for in 1483 Lord Hastings was beheaded by Richard III for treason, an event dramatically portrayed by Shakespeare in *King Richard III.*

In Main Street, practically opposite the approach to the church and next to the church hall, are some cottages designed by William Butterfield, built in 1859 to house workers at Castle Farm. The present primary school, built with a rather curious chimney in 1910, is in the back street called Barwell Road, but the original school of 1857 on the corner of Main Street and Ratby Lane is now a private house called Parson's Farewell. This half-timbered building – also designed by Butterfield – is now a coffee shop and a craft gallery, and is open several days a week.

To many enthusiasts this village is just the way to Mallory Park when there is motor-racing, but this noisy intrusion is a comparatively recent one and, as with so many other places, the story here begins at least as far back as Domesday Book and perhaps earlier. Fortunately the guide to All Saints church, Dorothy Fox's *The History of the Church and Parish of Kirkby Mallory*, includes a brief history of the village, the hall (now demolished) and the people – notably the Noels – who lived there. The guide is obtainable from the church once you have the key.

On the approach to both the park and the church gates, No 38 is the old school of 1863 which was closed in 1968 and is now the village hall. Note the coat of arms above an upstairs window. As you approach the church down a long drive, you cannot fail to see the free-standing memorial to Ada Augusta Lovelace, the daughter of the poet and adventurer Lord George Gordon Byron. The memorial was erected by her mother, Anne – the grand-daughter of Edward Noel, later Viscount Wentworth – who had married Lord Byron in 1815 but separated from him barely 12 months later. Ada Augusta was a brilliant mathematician and helped to evolve a system which was the forerunner of today's computers. She died in 1852 when only 36 years old.

The history and the contents of All Saints church are fully written up in the guide so I will only add a few features overlooked or not stressed in this. There is a sundial on a buttress on the south wall where the south doorway is blocked up, so the entrance to the church is by the north porch which was added in the 18th century when the north aisle was done away with. Note the date '1615' on the rector's stall in the chancel – in fact all the choir stalls are Jacobean and the wooden reredos is of an even earlier date and believed to be 16th century. The numerous memorials to the Noel family – particularly that of Sir William Noel, Bart, who died in 1675 – are all mentioned in the guide but what will catch the eye on first entering is the most unusual font where the figure of an angel is holding out a bowl!

KNIPTON AND HARSTON

——— Belvoir Castle, the home of the Dukes of Rutland, stands high on an isolated spur above the Vale of Belvoir and can be seen from many miles away. Clustered around the spur, these two neat villages have been the homes of the 'workers' on the estate for very many years. There is no need to elaborate on the castle because it is well known on the 'Stately Home' circuit, and particularly for the medieval jousting tournaments held there in the summer, so let us look at these estate villages.

In the centre of *Knipton* is an old pump by the little green between the post office and the old school of 1854. Along the road to Harston there are several early Victorian estate cottages which are dated and, where the road bends rather sharply, a lodge to the castle. All Saints church stands at the end of the short cul-de-sac above the old school and has several interesting features. In the porch a 13th century reredos is built into the east wall and is decorated with four flowers with a cross between the centre pair and various other ornaments. Also in the porch is a small alabaster stone showing the figure of a child in swaddling clothes with the inscription around it 'off your charite praye for the soul of John Eyre...' a sad memorial of 1558. Note also the 18 bench ends built into the stalls of the choir.

At *Harston*, along the road to Denton in Lincolnshire, there is Honeysuckle Cottage with a coat of arms on the wall, and the old school is dated 1868. Just north of the church is a house called Crossway which has a pump built into the wall facing the road. St Michael's church is down the turning to Croxton – I mention this because it is rather hidden compared to so many elsewhere – but, apart from the 14th century ironstone tower, both chancel and nave are late Victorian. There are, however, other relics of the past; in the east wall of the chancel there is an Anglo-Saxon stone and the font is 15th century. In the churchyard is the tomb of a Mary Parker who died in 1782.

KNOSSINGTON, OWSTON, COLD OVERTON AND LAUNDE

—— Two of these three villages, together with Launde Abbey, are on the western fringe of Rutland and so, even with Owston further to the west, it is geographically convenient to deal with them together. Ignored by Arthur Mee, *Knossington* has its place in Domesday Book as 'Closintone' and, as early as 1125, records show the spelling to be 'Knossintun' so it certainly has a long history despite this omission. The village is spread out around its open centre (Main Street) from which roads lead off to Cold Overton, Braunston, Somerby and Owston. Opposite the start of the Owston road is the old village pump.

In this centre is the village hall, formerly an old school, whilst a few yards down the Owston Road is the 1901 school, still with its bell and now a private house. Immediately opposite is Priory Farm (No 17) with a gateway reputedly from Owston Abbey (see below). Like the school, the post office has disappeared but a house a few doors back towards Main Street bears the legend The Old Post Office. Opposite here, on the corner of Owston Road and Main Street, is what was known as Knossington Hospital – actually a home built for the widows of retired clergymen. Founded in 1711 and rebuilt in 1820, this building also is now in private hands.

Back in the centre, at the junction of the Braunston and Cold Overton roads, is The Walnuts, a house with parts dated 1610 and on a bend in the road, at the start of The Hollow, is the Methodist chapel. The most interesting house in Main Street is No 15 built on the site of The Greyhound, a former public house which closed in 1930. The present house now has a garden in front but the owner very kindly showed me a turn-of-the-century photograph of the former public house and explained that the façade of the house facing the street was from Normanton Hall, demolished in 1925 (see *Empingham*). He told me that he installed the sundial over the door to celebrate the 200th anniversary of the Normanton façade!

At the start of Somerby Road, and on the bend out of Main Street, are the columns at the entrance to The Old Rectory – a typically large house of (probably) the 18th century, and round the corner is the remaining public house the Fox and Hounds and on the other side of the road St Peter's church. The ironstone west tower, not embattled but with gargoyles below the parapet is, according to Pevsner, c1400 although the tower arch could be earlier. The chancel and other parts are all the result of Blomfield's restoration work in 1882–83. Note, however, the 13th century font, the very slender octagonal arcade piers of the same period and the Perpendicular fragments of a screen at the east end of the south aisle. Continuing along Somerby Road is the entrance to The Grange, now a private remedial school for boys, and round the corner, along Somerby Road and on the edge of the grounds of The Grange is the attractive Dairy Cottage.

Before the almost universal use of the motor car *Owston*, west of Knossington, must have been a very remote village indeed, which could have been the reason for the founding of an abbey in 1161 by Robert Grimbald. No longer remote – although the roads do get narrower! The reason for a visit is St Andrew's church which is but a fragment of the former abbey. One approach is beside the former vicarage, now called The Priory, which reputedly has some arches and stones from the ruins of the abbey incorporated in the north and south walls.

South of the churchyard and mainly west of the village are the 'only tangible reminders of the Abbey's existence...terraced features in the fields probably indicating walls and boundary banks of the Abbey property and also the site of former fish-ponds'. This quote is from *Owston: a Short History* written in 1983 by J.D. Buchanan. On sale in the church, it is a fascinating document outlining the history and the demography of the village and, of course, it tells the story of the founding and the dissolution of the abbey.

There are only a few architectural notes about the church, which possibly just represents the original chancel and north chapel of the abbey church, so I will add my own comments. The south door is blocked so entry is by the north doorway of c1200 which is, actually, in the c1300 tower. This was built at the north-west corner instead of the west end because the ground slopes away quite steeply. In the north aisle there is a much-embellished recess in the north wall and nearby is a vestments table.

South-east of Owston is Withcote Hall and Chapel – in private hands although the chapel, like All Saints at Beeby, is in the care of the Churches Conservation Trust. A little further south-east is *Launde*, better known as *Launde Abbey*, which is the Diocesan Retreat House and Conference Centre. It is open on certain days of the year but over the August Bank Holiday weekend Launde, in the words of the Bishop of Leicester, 'opens itself up to "fun for all the family"'. Originally there was a priory here, founded between 1119 and 1125 and dissolved by Henry VIII. The present house, although much altered over the centuries, may have been built on the ruins. Note the ha-ha round the rectangular lawn in front of the house. Not quite between Withcote and Launde is the site of Sauvey Castle (the Ordnance map has it as 'Sanvey Castle') which Pevsner calls 'the finest Norman motte-and-bailey castle in the county'.

Cold Overton, about a mile to the north-east of Knossington and two miles west of Langham in Rutland, is celebrated not only for Cold Overton Hall – what Arthur Mee calls 'one of the finest houses in Leicestershire' and built, or at least completed, during the Restoration of Charles II – but also for the wall paintings in St John the Baptist church. The hall is now in private hands and the site of its former kitchen gardens a flourishing garden centre – probably much more celebrated locally today than the hall! The houses of the village are a mixture of brick and stone, and note particularly Court Farm beside the church with its octagonal dovecote in the farmyard. Opposite the farm is the Old Rectory which dates from the late 16th century. The village is now part of the Whatborough Group Parish and, according to the WI Village Book, no rector has lived in the village since 1900.

There is *A Brief History of the Church* in St John's so I will just mention features which are not, or barely touched on in the guide. The wall paintings in the chapel at the eastern end of the south aisle are included but, apart from a couple of lines about the carvings on the tower, there is hardly a mention of the wealth of carved heads, beasts and grotesques to be found all over this church. Entry is by the south porch and note where this has been cut back to fit in one of the two figures of what the guide says is 'the oldest feature...the inner doorway'. This Early English portal, which 'may have been taken from the original south wall and reused when the aisle was added' is flanked by columns and lavishly decorated by fleurons over the top. As you leave, do not miss the sundial above the porch entrance.

LEIRE AND FROLESWORTH

——— Whatever its medieval origins, the village of *Leire* is pronounced as in 'King Lear', confirmed by locals in the village post office in Main Street when I asked about its age. There was less certainty about the age of the post office – apparently early 19th century – but everyone was happy to impress me with the correct pronunciation of 'Leire'.

Also in Main Street is Glebe House dated 1793, which was used during the 19th century for the making of Stilton cheese. The old school is now the village hall, and there is the Wesleyan chapel of 1863. Opposite St Peter's church is the timber-framed and thatched manor house, the oldest house in the village. St Peter's church has a Perpendicular tower but the rest was rebuilt in 1867–68, just as at Shawell and by the same William Smith using several similar features. There is a sundial on one of the buttresses of the tower, which has battlements and gargoyles.

Leaving Leire westward over the dismantled railway – where there is now a nature walk – you come to *Frolesworth* and in view immediately are the Plough inn and the almshouses founded by John Smith, who was born in the village and became Lord Chief Baron of the Exchequer in Scotland. He never forgot his birthplace and made provision in his will for an almshouse. A plaque at the gate gives the details and records that the original building was completed in 1761, adding that major improvements were carried out in 1965.

Amongst the period houses in the village is the Old Vicarage with wrought-iron gates between brick gate piers topped by knob finials. Opposite is St Nicholas church where Baron John Smith is buried and his story is told on a large upright slab set into the south wall of the chancel. By the chancel arch are the remains of a stairway and the blocked opening to a rood loft; note that the south aisle with its octagonal piers is much narrower than the north aisle which has circular piers.

Perhaps the most interesting features here are the two altar tombs on either side of the altar. On the south side is the tomb of Francis Staresmore who died in 1626 and this monument, the sculpted recumbent effigy of him in full armour together with the effigies of his 11 children by both his wives, was erected by his second wife, Frances (née Brocas) in 1631. Her own tomb is on the north side of the altar; Frances lived until 1657 and her tomb was erected the following year with her effigy shown lying in a shroud.

LONG CLAWSON

—— Long Clawson certainly lives up to its name, though as the WI Village Book tells us, centuries ago possibly there were two distinct settlements. As you approach the village from Melton Mowbray, via either Holwell or Scalford, an old tower windmill is visible at Mill Farm, about a mile to the south. This can be seen from either of the two parallel roads which, on the map, make a sandwich of the very long Long Clawson.

The church is in the west end of the village and almost diagonally opposite is the 17th century manor house with a pump in the garden. Behind it is a well maintained village pond. Shops and two chapels are all in the east end, and the Dairy Company produce their well-known Stilton cheese.

The ironstone church is dedicated, unusually, to St Remigius (there are only four other churches so dedicated in the country and three are in Norfolk) and, although there are some Norman remains, much of the church is early 14th century including the central tower with battlements. The porch also has battlements and part of a sundial. The stone altar under a wooden frame has an inscription recording that it was given in 1737, and in the south transept is the late 13th century mutilated stone effigy of a cross-legged knight. Originally in the north chapel, according to the *Memorials of Old Leicestershire* it suffered 'many years of bad usage by children when the chapel was used as a village school'!

LUBENHAM

Lubenham lies on the busy A417 road between Market Harborough and Lutterworth. Variously labelled 'Lubanham', 'Lubeham' or 'Lobenho' in Domesday Book, the village is very ancient, with remains of simply defended earthworks of the Ancient Britons. The modern Gartree Prison, built on the site of a World War Two airfield, lies just to the north.

The village, close by the county boundary with Northamptonshire, has little of hidden interest but All Saints church – practically on the boundary – is a gem. First note Tower House, built in 1860, which stands beside the gate into the churchyard; this could almost be called a folly structure! Full of architectural treasures, this church is kept locked, but a key can be obtained from a cottage in a narrow road just to the east of the churchyard. The church was in the throes of a major resuscitation when I visited but all the features which made it so interesting were soon to be put back in place – three-decker pulpit, numbered box pews and some 15th century bench ends with poppyheads, all combining to retain the church's 18th century air.

My key led me straight into the vestry which in reality is the north chapel. There is a c1300 sedilia and piscina and, strangely, a large Norman corbel from a corbel-table; also a squint. Other features include a large recess in the north wall of the chancel, possibly an Easter sepulchre, remains of the rood loft and wall paintings over the pulpit and on the south side of the chancel arch. One final feature here: a pier of 1190–1200 in the north arcade has a fascinating square capital with three grotesque faces peering out from among oak leaves.

MARKFIELD AND ULVERSCROFT

Three interpretations concerning the derivation of the name *Markfield* ('Merdefeld' in Domesday Book) are in front of me – 'open field by or with a pool', '"March Boundary" an open place or cleared area on the edge of the forest' being two of them – but neither is relevant to its present state. Nineteenth century quarrying accelerated any lingering idea that the village was in the Charnwood Forest, and in the middle of that century it was noted for the number of stocking framework-knitters – some 153 according to an 1844 return.

The old National school of 1851 and the Congregational church of a year later are still standing. On the hill above the Green is the church of St Michael, where a great deal of restoration, including the rebuilding of the chancel, was carried out in 1865 but its history dates back to at least 1215. Remains of some Norman zigzag work, probably from a former doorway, can be seen in the south wall of the nave. Note the blocked leper window on the south aisle wall. In the church a welcoming pamphlet sets out times of services and other activities, and also records the interesting fact that John Wesley preached here 13 times between 1741 and 1779.

I have bracketed these two places together solely because Markfield is the nearest place of any size, not to a village because there is none, but to the scattered community of cottages which stand within an area a few miles north-east of that village and the A50 and, above all, the *Ulverscroft* Priory founded by the Augustinian canons in 1134. Called by Arthur Mee 'perhaps the loveliest ruin in the county' and by Hoskins 'the largest monastic ruin in the county', the remains of the priory, originally built in the midst of Charnwood

Forest, stand near a farmhouse but, unfortunately, as Hoskins says 'visitors are not much encouraged'.

MEDBOURNE, DRAYTON AND NEVILL HOLT

—— The road from Great Easton to Medbourne goes right through the little village of *Drayton* – not to be confused with Fenny Drayton where George Fox, the founder of the Quakers, was born. Here on the village green, barely a mile from the border with Northamptonshire, the church of St James, which was 'formerly a Chapel of Ease within the neighbouring Parish of Bringhurst' is the smallest consecrated church in Leicestershire. It is all that remains of a Norman church and Hoskins recalls that a historian of the late 18th century mentioned that it had 'long been desecrated...[and] is now converted into a bake-house'. The nave, not much bigger than many living-rooms, was saved in 1878 and restored to its original purpose. The full story can be read on a memorial plaque on the green, one of several erected in the area in 1977 to celebrate the silver jubilee of Queen Elizabeth II.

After arriving in *Medbourne*, the first building you see at the beginning of the road to Ashley will be the old stables of the Fernie Hunt, now converted into flats. Bear right at the fork and almost immediately you arrive at the car park of the Nevill Arms. Do mind the ducks which frequent the brook separating the car park from the inn itself (access is by a small footbridge). They are so used to being fed that it is a very real hazard driving away, I had to get out of my car to check whether any were behind me! A hundred yards or so upstream is Medbourne's architectural treasure – a medieval packhorse bridge over the brook (which drains into the river Welland further south) and here you will find another memorial plaque – like the one at Drayton – giving the full story of the bridge.

The packhorse bridge lies between several old houses, one being The Shieling, and St Giles church – in fact, a path from the church leads straight on to the bridge. St Giles has a very

Medieval packhorse bridge, Medbourne.

lop-sided look but first I must quote an illuminated sign just inside the south door: 'On Jan 1st 1990 Her Majesty Queen Elizabeth II, by an Order in Council, decreed that the benefices of Bringhurst, cum Great Easton and Drayton, be amalgamated with the benefices of Medbourne cum Holt, Stockerston and Blaston, to form the new parish of The Six Saints circa Holt.'

St Giles appears lop-sided because there is an extensive south aisle, but no north aisle; as Pevsner says it looks as if it had been 'left incomplete'. In the south transept, off the south aisle and under an ogee arch, is a much mutilated effigy which *Memorials of Old Leicestershire* says 'probably represents the founder of the transept'. Note the 13th century sedilia in the south wall and in the chancel, rebuilt in 1876, another stepped sedilia. Note also the huge clock pendulum hanging down in the tower and the 13th century drum-shaped font.

Before leaving the area, take the little road with a signpost pointing to *Nevill Holt*, over the track of the dismantled railway and after a mile or so you come upon a magnificent building and the church of St Mary. Holt is a 'deserted village' but when the mansion – with a history going back to the 14th century – was enlarged by the Nevill family (hence the 'Nevill Arms') the whole park took on the name of Nevill Holt. From 1876 to 1912 the estate was owned by the Cunard shipping family but in 1919 it became a preparatory school so you can only stand at the main gate and have a good look.

NETHER BROUGHTON AND OLD DALBY

Like Ab Kettleby, its near neighbour south of Broughton Hill on the same stretch of the A606, the village of *Nether Broughton* is hidden from the traveller who only gets a rather drab view of the place when en route for the Nottinghamshire border less than a mile away. Even in this small place, a one-way traffic system is in operation so take the only route possible and head for St Mary's church which lies right on the northern edge of the village overlooking the Vale of Belvoir.

Passing Hecadeck Cottage dated 1762 and nearly opposite another cottage with a plaque 'FA 1773' over the door, you arrive at the church with gate pillars engraved with the words 'In Memory of Sir Winston Churchill 1874–1965'. At the church, normally kept locked, cleaners made quite sure that I did not miss a small panel high up on the south wall of the south aisle depicting a lamb with a flag; there is also a Saxon stone in the vestry. Look upwards in the nave where you will find eight stone angels playing musical instruments – corbels supporting the roof.

Outside, the tower, like many in this area, has a quatre-foiled lozenge frieze below the embattled top; there are also gargoyles and pinnacles. Many gravestones are of Swithland slate; note particularly the wording on one beside the path to the gate:

'Stephen Hopkins who fell asleep in Jesus
Dec 14 1846 Aged 47 years.
Also Sarah, his wife, who departed this life
for a joyful immortality
Jan 14 1869 Aged 64 years'.

To return to the main road, follow the one-way route. Just before returning to the A606 there is a Wesleyan chapel dated 1839; another panel indicates that it was renovated in 1889.

Turn south again on to the main road but follow the signs for *Old Dalby* almost immediately. A minor road, after passing a RAOC tank repair depot (scheduled to be closed) will bring you to the village which, by rights, should be called 'Dalby-on-the-Wolds'. The first building of note is the undated Wesleyan chapel at the end of Chapel Lane. On the southern edge of the village is the church of St John the Baptist which was completely rebuilt in 1835 but has retained inside the 16th century tomb chests and effigies of several of the Noel family. Beside the path from the gate is the tombstone of one Edward Purdey who died in 1743 and the sad story of how he met his death can clearly be read in rhyming couplets. St John's lies between two ruined gateways to the hall, now converted into private residences. Opposite the church gate is Home Farm built in 1835, contemporary with the building of the church.

NEWTON HARCOURT, KILBY AND WISTOW

The WI Village Book tells us that 'the history of Newton Harcourt is inevitably linked with Wistow Hall' and that 'In the 19th century much of the village (Kilby) was part of the Wistow estate' so it seems natural to bracket these three places together.

Newton Harcourt lies between the A6 and the A50, and, although it is the first village south of the spreading conurbation of Leicester, which has already swallowed up Oadby and Wigston, it appears very tranquil, even though it is separated from the Grand Union Canal by the railway line from Market Harborough. One of the little cul-de-sacs off Glen Road (the road through the village) is called the Square where at one time there was an inn and other buildings useful to the community. These are all private houses now but outside No 3 an old pump has been preserved. The old school house of 1866 is down Middle Lane, another cul-de-sac, and opposite, on the other side of Glen Road, is Octagon Cottage – an eight-sided former toll house of the 18th century.

Immediately south of the rail and canal bridges is the very small St Luke's church with a 13th century tower but both the nave and the chancel are of 1834. It does, however, retain a font dated 1777. In the churchyard note the monument – possibly unique – in the shape of a miniature church set up in memory of a boy of eight. Set back from the road, but more or less opposite the church, is the manor house. Once a dower house, it is mainly of the early 17th century but has 19th century alterations which, according to Pevsner, were probably made by Joseph Goddard who lived there and died in 1900. He was responsible for much of the church restoration work in the county and for one or two new churches (see *Tur Langton*).

South of the church the road leads to *Wistow*, shortened from 'Wistanstowe' – holy place of Wistan – and the attractive church dedicated to St Wistan who was martyred here in AD 847 and later canonised. The site of the old medieval village is shown on the Ordnance map and now all that remains, apart from the church, is Wistow Hall and its lake, and a garden centre together with Wistan le Dale – its model village. The hall, at present the home of the Lord Lieutenant of the county, has a long history – particularly with Charles I both before and after the battle of Naseby – but you can read all about it and the church in two admirable pamphlets available at St Wistan's after obtaining the key at the hall.

Although the pamphlets contain a lot of history and details of the various personalities over the years, I must add that the church is one of the very few in the county to retain box pews and a two-decker pulpit, and that Sir Henry Halford, who inherited Wistow in 1814, was the King's Physician and attended George III, George IV and William IV. He is reputed to have realised that George III was suffering from the hereditary disease of porphyria and not mad at all!

Drive away from Wistow over the cattle grids in a westerly direction and you come to *Kilby* where the Langham Memorial United Reformed church ('Bequeathed by and In Memory of John Langham, Nottingham') is situated half-way down Main Street. The parish church of St Mary Magdalene, built in 1858, stands somewhat isolated at the extreme west end of the village. The nave and chancel are all in one and there is a small bellcote. Across the A50 and on the Countesthorpe road is a signpost which points to '10th Century Church'. I drove down the narrow road past Foston Hall Farm to St Bartholomew's which used to be the church of *Foston*, another deserted village but it was locked, with no indication as to whether the church was still in use although there was a mention that keys were to be obtained in Countesthorpe. I felt, however, that the sign to what is perhaps the oldest church in the county was sadly misleading.

NEWTOWN LINFORD AND BRADGATE PARK

——— Newtown Linford is one of the county's prettiest villages – only two miles or so from Anstey but you will notice a complete contrast immediately. It consists mainly of one main street, except for the houses along the Groby Road, but in it there are a number of cruck, timber-framed and other attractive cottages. That is not all: as Arthur Mee puts it 'The village is the doorstep to Bradgate Park' and, unfortunately, the car park for the Park is situated right in the middle of the village, with its attendant problems.

Between All Saints Church and the turning for Markfield at the north-west end of the village there is cruck-built Vine Cottage, Gable Cottage, Rose Cottage and others. Some of these timber-framed houses are thatched, some roofed with Swithland slates but all are of the 16th or 17th century. The church is approached through a lychgate and once inside, you are made aware of the tragic story of Lady Jane Grey, whose childhood home was Bradgate House in the park. There is an excellent guide available so I will just emphasise a few features. Firstly, in the chancel arch is the unusual tympanum carrying the painted royal arms of the House of Hanover flanked by the arms of the Grey family. Secondly, note the slab of Swithland slate covered in the alphabet and numerals. Finally, outside again, search for the remains of the two 14th century scratch dials – at the base of the tower and east of the porch on the south wall.

The church is on one side of the Bradgate car park and on the east side, just before the car park, there is a little building on which can be seen the words 'Sunday School 1822'. Bradgate Park, once the home of the Grey family, is the only large area of land in the county that has never been cultivated or even artificially landscaped. After Charles Bennion bought the estate in 1928 he presented it, as the memorial to him in the park states, 'In trust for the City and County of Leicester that for all time it might be preserved in its natural state for the quiet enjoyment of the people of Leicestershire. His true memorial lies around'.

The ruins of Bradgate House are not open to the public but they can be seen from the park, and there is a visitor centre showing dioramic displays on Lady Jane Grey and her nine days as queen, also on the Bradgate House ruins and other aspects of the area. At the highest point of the park there is the folly known as 'Old John' erected in 1786. Various stories exist about its origin but it would appear that the fifth Earl of Stamford erected it to the memory of an old retainer who was killed accidentally at the spot. Not far from 'Old John' is the 1914–18 war memorial to the Leicestershire Yeomanry.

NORTH KILWORTH AND SOUTH KILWORTH

The benefices of both parishes became one in 1962, with one rector living at North Kilworth so, naturally, these two villages close to the Northamptonshire border, joined by the B5414, must be dealt with together.

The first thing to notice about *North Kilworth* – immediately south of the A427 – is that unlike most other villages there are no names to the streets. Right next to St Andrew's church is the old rectory, now a nursing home, and just north of the church is the Belgrave memorial hall of 1902. The Belgraves have lived in the parish since the 14th century and, except for a short break in the middle, they provided the rectors for the church from 1701 right through to 1901. There is a helpful guide in the church so all I need do is add a few further details. Before entering by the north doorway have a look for the stone owl on the battlements of the tower. Inside, note that there are no capitals on the piers of the north arcade – quite unlike the south aisle built during the heavy restoration work of 1864.

South Kilworth is two miles south-west of the other Kilworth down the B5414, and stands where that road crosses the link between Northampton and Lutterworth just to the north of the Stanford reservoir. Its most famous resident was William Pearson, rector here from 1821 until his death in 1847. He was also a pioneer of the Royal Institution and a founder member of the Royal Astronomical Society. As he could not house his telescope in the (former) 18th century rectory, he built an observatory in the village on what is now the B5414. This is now a private dwelling but the original octagonal shape can still be seen. At the beginning of Welford Road is the South Kilworth Congregational church.

Pearson is buried in the middle of the northern part of the churchyard, and he is commemorated inside St Nicholas church by an attractive wall plaque decorated with, amongst other embellishments, a miniature telescope. Available in the church is a leaflet photocopy reproducing an illustration from John Nichol's famous 18th century *History and Antiquities of the County of Leicester* and on the reverse side explanatory detail. No mention is made of the major restoration work undertaken in 1868–69 when the chancel and the aisles were replaced. The ceiling of the chancel was restored and repainted again in 1984.

Outside, on the south face of the tower above the porch is a statue of St Nicholas in a niche which escaped the attentions of Cromwell's men, and inside the 13th century font, shaped like a Corinthian capital, has survived all the changes and restorations of the last two centuries. Now for the real treasure of this church which is the Wythnale tomb reproduced on the leaflet. Both Arthur Mee in 1937 and Pevsner describe a 'reredos' in the north aisle, in Mee's case incorrectly. There is an effigy of a priest in a recess in the sanctuary believed to be the top of the tomb of Richard Wythnale who died in 1439. The so-called 'reredos' is the side panel of this tomb – depicting what is known as a rare 'Lily' crucifix and flanked by the Angel Gabriel (John, according to Mee) and Mary – which, for centuries, was in the north aisle. Now, and I am indebted to the present incumbent for all this information, the panel has been positioned on the east wall of the south aisle and *only now* is it a reredos in the little chapel there.

PACKINGTON

—— Cut off from Ashby-de-la-Zouch by the A42 trunk road, the compact village of Packington is, no doubt, thankful that it is spared many of the juggernaut lorries which might otherwise be thundering through it. Consequently it is that much easier to have a look at a brick octagonal lock-up, even though it is somewhat overshadowed by a nearby house. One of only three in the county, it is tucked into the side of one of the village's fairly quiet roads. It still has a strong door and an octagonal pointed roof surmounted by a finial.

Holy Rood church is very nearly the last building on the south-west of the village on the road to Measham. Set back from the road, entrance is gained by the unusual north door. Much rebuilding took place early in the 19th century but basically it is of the 13th century and there are some bench ends reputedly of circa 1350. Another unusual feature can be found outside: six steps leading up to the exterior base of the west window.

PEATLING MAGNA AND WILLOUGHBY WATERLEYS

—— These two villages lie parallel to each other, roughly just north of the minor roads which link Arnesby and Broughton Astley, but similarly south of the Leicester conurbation, so I am linking them together. Both these villages are listed in Domesday Book but *Peatling Magna* is believed to date from the first century, making it one of the oldest settlements in the county. Much of the village is comparatively modern but Holly Tree Farm, at the beginning of Church Lane, has a chequered arrangement of bricks and is probably of the 18th century: opposite is The Cock Inn and the Coronation Memorial Hall of 1911.

All Saints church, which dates mainly from the 13th century, holds a lot of interest but as no guide is available, I must list what there is to see. First, outside, there is the base of an old cross in the churchyard and, looking at the tower with its short spire, note the typical Leicestershire battlements and pinnacles. The real interest of this church lies inside because of the furnishings, mainly of the 17th century, and the monuments to three different members of the Jervis family – all called William – who all died between 1597 and 1618.

In the north wall of the sanctuary there is a recess, probably an Easter Sepulchre, with a trefoiled arch and a coat of arms above it. In the chancel are first the tomb chest of William Jervis, who died in 1597, and his wife Katherine with their inscribed figures on the top slab with 18 children sculpted below. Second, under a 13th century arch on the north side, the tomb chest of William Jervis, who died in 1614, and his two wives, Anne and Frances, again with their inscribed figures on top of the slab but with only five sculpted children below. The monument to the other William Jervis, who died in 1618, is a wall monument and it bears the reminder: 'As you are so were we; as we are so shall you be'. The reredos and the pulpit, together with a complete tester, are both of 1685 but the bench ends in the nave – note the decorated bases – are probably all of 1604: you will find that date on one of them. Even earlier than that are two pre-Reformation benches preserved at the back of the church and two poppyheads of the same period are in the choir.

To the west is *Willoughby Waterleys* (some reference books have the second half of the name as Waterless) which lies between two branches of the Whetstone Brook and is certainly not 'waterless'! St Mary's church is also basically 13th century but was substantially restored in 1875 when the chancel was rebuilt. There is a Norman font from an earlier church, and the piscina together with a double sedilia are of the 13th century but renewed. In the village, the former 1877 Primitive Methodist chapel is now a private house and the old school of 1846 is now the village hall which stands beside the General Elliott inn.

Apart from two cul-de-sacs this is a one-street village which both Pevsner and Hoskins describe as 'exceptionally rich in dated or dateable brick houses'. Next to the church is the old rectory of 1740 (with 'The Leys' on the gatepost) where there is a church key-holder. On the opposite side of the road is Manor Farm of 1693 with a fine entrance flanked by gateposts with stone vases. Further down is a cottage dated 1731 and then The Limes of 1702 and again gateposts with vases. Finally, a short distance to the south of the village is the Old Hall – older than all of them – probably dated late 16th century and once again there are gateposts with vases.

PEATLING PARVA, BRUNTINGTHORPE, WALTON, KIMCOTE AND GILMORTON

These five villages, listed in clockwise order, are situated around the former Bruntingthorpe Airfield and Proving Ground and so make a natural grouping although Gilmorton is, for our purposes, the most interesting. *Peatling*

Parva, arguably slightly larger than its Magna namesake, lies immediately north of the runway. The inside of St Andrew's church remained hidden to me because this is one of those very few locked churches where I was unable to find out who held the key. The Perpendicular tower has the typical local appearance with battlements, gargoyles and a frieze of pointed quatrefoils enclosing shields but no pinnacles.

St Mary's church at *Bruntingthorpe* was rebuilt in 1873 apart from the lower parts of the tower which date back to the 12th century, and in its quiet cul-de-sac there are the old rectory and a restored coach-house. In Main Street there are several period houses set back with walled gardens, but the restored 18th century tithe barn of White House Farm is situated right alongside the street. Note also the former Baptist chapel of 1846 and the 1871 school which is now the village hall.

According to the WI Village Book there used to be a church at *Walton* but it became defunct circa 1630. Today, there is no church and so Walton and Kimcote combine to form one parish. Two other religious buildings are shown on the 1988 Ordnance map; the Wesleyan Baptist chapel of 1885 and a Mission chapel of 1886, listed by Pevsner but now demolished and the site of a private house. The church of this combined parish is the mainly late 13th century All Saints at *Kimcote* and opposite is the Old Rectory dated c1700. There is a bridleway marked on the map indicating a track southwards from the village to Great Poultney Farm, the site of the deserted village of Poultney.

And so along Kimcote Lane, to complete the encirclement of the former airfield, to *Gilmorton* where there is an excellent *Historic Village Trail* pamphlet – similar to others prepared by the District of Harborough – available in All Saints church. This pamphlet not only lists the many interesting period buildings in Main Street and the Lutterworth Road but gives their dates and a little history concerning each. Note particularly Tansley's Thatch next to the village hall, and Tudor Cottage – both probably of the 16th century although the second one is no longer thatched. All Saints church, with its porch built to celebrate Queen Victoria's Diamond Jubilee in

1897, is another church noted for its Kempe stained glass (see *Sheepy Magna*).

QUENIBOROUGH AND SYSTON

—— *Queniborough* is another village along or adjacent to the A607, with a history stretching back beyond the Norman Conquest – Saxon bygones have been unearthed here – but, after a thousand years and only seven miles from the city, it now more or less consists of the wide main street leading to the church and, as in so many places, modern housing estates. In what could be called the centre of the village, at the end of School Lane and practically on top of one another are the two public houses, the Britannia inn and the Horse and Groom. Also in the lane is the old National school of 1847.

Going down the main street towards St Mary's church several houses or cottages of different periods claim attention, because of their date or some architectural feature. Note particularly the cruck side wall of a cottage nearly opposite the Britannia inn, No 86 which is dated 1730, No 79 dated 1703, a stone house diagonally across from the church has two very large chimney stacks and just across from the east end of the church is a house of c1820 with castellations. Around the bend in the continuation of Main Street is Queniborough New Hall where there used to be a dovecote dated 1705, restored and re-sited 1987/1988 in the paddock behind the church.

And so to St Mary's church with its superb spire which, according to the church guide, 'is said to be the second highest in the county'. As this very comprehensive guide covers not only the architectural features of the church and its history, but also the past living conditions of clergy and parishioners I need only add a few additional notes. Note the opening high up on the north side of the chancel arch indicating that there was a rood loft here but the rood screen – restored in circa 1920 – is now at the back of the church. The font, the pulpit, the carved roof timbers in the nave and the spire are described in the guide, but note also the locally typical frieze, battlements and gargoyles on the tower. I must record the first thing to catch my eye as I entered: a large banner which read '7 Days Without Prayer Make One Weak'.

A mile or so to the south-west is *Syston* where the only historic interest lies in one or two houses in Church Street and one dated 1686 in Brook Street, but do take a look at Wreake Valley College on the north side of the town: from a distance it gives the impression of being a cruise liner! St Peter and St Paul church, with its wealth of carving, has a great deal of interest. At the time of my visit there was no guide available, though a new one was planned, but I was fortunate in that the vicar was in the church when I visited and he pointed out at least one feature which I would have missed. The sedilia in the chancel is of the 13th century, and I was shown remnants of a Saxon cross discovered built into the top of it: this was indeed a hidden artefact!

All the piers, the arches of the aisles and the tower arch are unusual in that they are all panelled, and the clerestory windows have panelled jambs as well, but the nave carving and the aisle corbels are the chief points of interest. In the north aisle there are six angels playing musical instruments and in the south the corbels are more floral in design. Twelve wooden figures – all brightly coloured – in the nave roof all bear similarly coloured shields. All these roof carvings are reputed to have been executed by monks of Ulverscroft Priory some time between 1350 and the Reformation. Outside, the tower has the usual battlements, pinnacles, gargoyles, also a quatrefoiled lozenge frieze found in these parts, and there is a tomb recess in the outside wall of the south aisle.

QUORN OR QUORNDON

────── The Ordnance map shows it as 'Quorndon' with 'Quorn' only in brackets but, despite the medieval derivation of the name – 'the hill (don) where millstones (or querns) were obtained' – it is the Quorn Hunt, after more than 200 years and much recent publicity, which virtually dictates the name of this large village (small town?) so let us settle for the shorter version.

The A6 trunk road has bypassed the village now and the reduced traffic on the old road certainly allows less dangerous sight-seeing; so, on driving from the direction of Leicester, we begin with the old brick chimney in the factory on the right which dominates the scene. My first reaction was that it had been retained only in the interests of industrial archaeology but was told that Wrights factory – which produced much of the webbing equipment in the two World Wars – was still very active. On the other side of the old road, down Meeting Street, is Quorn House. The present building dates from only about 1820 but this was the seat of the Farnham family from c1284. There is also Quorn Hall which was built by another Farnham in c1680, but this now belongs to Loughborough University.

There are a few period houses here including early 19th century Quorn Court to the west of the High Street but, on the other side of the High Street, we need only concern ourselves with St Bartholomew's, a united Anglican and Methodist church. This granite building, which survived a disastrous fire in 1965, has parts which are of Norman origin but the most interesting feature is the Farnham chapel in the south aisle, containing memorials and tombs of the family. I need only add a few notes because there is a very comprehensive guide on sale in the church which deals thoroughly with the history of the fabric and the bells. The guide does not mention the five decorated bosses in the nave roof nor the five corbels supporting it on each side. Finally, note what the guide calls a finger dial – elsewhere referred to as a mass or scratch dial (see *Great Easton* and *Ratcliffe-on-the-Wreake*) – which, having been moved from a lower position, is now on a buttress to the right of the locked entrance door to the Farnham chapel.

I cannot leave Quorn without mentioning one of the big local, and certainly not hidden, tourist attractions. Steam trains run on eight miles of preserved main line of the old

Great Central Railway between Loughborough and Leicester North via Quorn and Rothley. There are 18 preserved locomotives and trains run every weekend, and daily in the height of the summer – to the delight of young and old.

RAVENSTONE

On the edge of the former coalfields, and what can be loosely described as situated between Coalville and Ashby-de-la-Zouch, the village of Ravenstone has one outstanding feature: the remarkably large almshouse group founded by Rebecca Wilkins in 1711 in memory of her son. The foundation inscription is above the main entrance recording this fact so do not be confused by the inscription over a doorway facing Hospital Lane. This reads 'In grateful and affectionate memory of John Turner, Knight Bachelor'; he was responsible for installing electricity in the establishment.

East of the almshouses is St Michael's church mainly of the early 14th century with a low tower and short broach-spire. In the south aisle is a crudely carved head of John the Baptist but otherwise there is not much to excite our interest. In the churchyard the war memorial carries the unusual wording: 'In Glorious Memory of the Unreturning Brave'.

REARSBY, THRUSSINGTON AND RATCLIFFE-ON-THE-WREAKE

Elsewhere in this book, several villages are grouped together due to close proximity. These three also qualify for a grouping linked as they are by the river Wreake and on either side of the Melton to Leicester railway line.

Rearsby is not on the Wreake, but a brook which flows through the village alongside Brook Street does finally join the river. To reach St Michael's church from Brook Street you have to cross this brook by a seven-arched packhorse bridge on foot – by car you will have to ford it! – and then walk up a slight incline. Although the WI book mentions that it was built in 1714, Pevsner and others maintain that the bridge is medieval and it certainly looks it. In Brook Street is the school dating back to 1872 and in the main road the Methodist church of 1849. No 2 Mill Street – known as Rearsby Old Hall – is dated 1661 and further down the street part of No 8 is even earlier, being dated 1610.

The tower of St Michael's church is typical of so many in this area – battlements, pinnacles and gargoyles but without the quatrefoiled frieze. Mainly of the 13th century it was heavily restored twice in Victorian times. Note particularly the sedilia in the chancel and the drum-shaped font – these are both of the 13th century. Return to Brook Street and take the road leading to Thrussington on the left past the school. Just before crossing the railway note the sign indicating the entrance to the Convent of Sisters of St Joseph of Peace. At the crossing is the 1846 station which has been converted into a private house.

Holy Trinity church is very visible as you enter *Thrussington* having crossed over the river Wreake – no ancient bridge here – but it is right and right again before you find it at the very end of Church Lane. Although small, it has the look of so many local churches – built of ironstone with pinnacles and gargoyles on the tower – but heavily restored in 1877. The interest in this village lies in the vernacular building and note first the large house opposite the end of Church Lane. There is a thatched cottage with '1723' picked out in black bricks and on No 15 Ratcliffe Road is a plaque which reads:

W & J Derby
1854
HITHERTO THE LORD HATH
HELPED US

Further along the Ratcliffe Road is the Old Manor House of c1700 with a dovecote in the grounds dated 1716.

Continue along the Ratcliffe Road and you arrive at *Ratcliffe-on-the-Wreake*, the third village in this triangle sandwiched between the river and Fosse Way (A46). On the west side of the trunk road is the well-known Roman Catholic college and south of the village is Shipley Hill, shown on the Ordnance map. For many years this was thought to be a Neolithic barrow but it has now been established as a natural spur shaped through the centuries by weather and farming.

St Botolph's church is kept locked but a card tells you of the whereabouts of the key. The first thing to notice is that the chancel is lower than the nave. There are no aisles now but there was a north aisle until 1795 and the blocked up arches of the arcade can still be seen. A triple sedilia and piscina in the chancel date it as early 14th century and the font is of the same period or even earlier. There is a tomb with an effigy of a priest in the sanctuary although the features are much defaced, and the roof is supported by ten corbels with floral decorations. Note the stone in the wall above the pulpit which bears the date 1310 and finally, as you leave the porch which was rebuilt in 1967, note the scratch dial on an outside window sill.

ROTHERBY, BROOKSBY AND HOBY

—— Like *Frisby*, Rotherby and Hoby are villages in the valley of the river Wreake whilst Brooksby – once the home of George Villiers, 1st Duke of Buckingham – is an agricultural college. As they are so near to each other they can be covered together.

If you take the A607 road after visiting Frisby-on-the-Wreake, you will pass what is shown as 'Stump Cross' on the Ordnance map, but the quickest way to *Rotherby* is by the minor road after turning left at the Bell in Frisby. There is nothing of unusual interest here; All Saints church is mainly 14th century although a blocked Norman window in the west wall of the nave is evidence of an earlier church. The tower is typical of many locally with pinnacles, gargoyles and, above all, a quatrefoiled lozenge frieze below the battlements.

Immediately to the west of the church, and running parallel

with the railway to the north and the A607 to the south, a gated road leads over a picturesque common to the County Agricultural College consisting of a variety of buildings which originated basically with the hall at *Brooksby*. The college is not open to the public. For the fascinating story of the various residents of the Hall read the WI Village Book and others listed in the Bibliography. St Michael's church is in the grounds of the hall but on a visit I was unable to find the keyholder. The tower has the local battlements and frieze as at Rotherby and elsewhere.

Take the only road and as you drive over the railway at the level-crossing you will see the derelict railway station of 1846. Straight after that you cross the river Wreake and drive up a hill to *Hoby*. There are a number of timber-framed buildings here – in particular the cruck Rose Tree Cottage. The Hoby Methodist church is in Chapel Lane but the ironstone All Saints church dominates the village; the key can be obtained from Church View opposite. There is the base and part of a shaft of an old cross in the churchyard and note the 1744 church wardens' names on a guttering on the outside of the south wall. Inside there are some poppyhead benches of c1500, and a large coat of arms of George III on the west wall over the organ. Features in the south aisle are a stepped sedilia with a piscina and a brass of the lower half of a knight in armour c1480, and an altar table with 13th century supports and dogtooth or nailhead strips.

Two miles or so to the north of Hoby is *Ragdale* where at one time there were two halls – Old Hall and New Hall. The Old Hall of 1629–1630 was demolished in 1958 but the New Hall of 1785, with its tower, is now a well-known hydro.

SADDINGTON

—— Though not as well known as the nearly two mile long Blisworth tunnel further south, the half mile Saddington tunnel carrying the Grand Union Canal starts just north of where the canal goes under the road leading from Smeeton Westerby to Saddington at just about the half way point. It was built in 1797 when canals were the main highway for transporting goods but now the canal only carries pleasure craft, and the tunnel is noted for its population of bats. South of the village is a reservoir which was built in the same decade as the tunnel for the purpose of feeding the canal.

In the village the brick Baptist chapel of 1848 stands next to Yew Tree House, and nearby is the old school house of 1855 – now a private house – opposite the Queen's Head inn next door to the old rectory. Entrance to St Helen's church is by the 13th century north doorway where there are two statues, male and female, standing upright on either side of the doorway: these were brought from an unknown church elsewhere. The church was, Pevsner writes, 'heavily and unsympathetically restored' in 1872–73, but note the angels on both sides of the chancel arch.

SAXBY AND STAPLEFORD

There is no village at Stapleford, and Saxby is only a tiny hamlet, but they are linked by their churches. St Peter's at Saxby (1789) and St Mary Magdalene at Stapleford (1783) were both built by George Richardson who was commissioned by Robert Sherard, the 4th Earl of Harborough.

St Peter's at *Saxby* is an austere, small, neo-classical building and, as Pevsner says 'the whole is an attempt at combining the tradition of the Hawksmoor churches of London with Leicestershire usage'. The unusual tower is the dominating feature with four vases instead of pinnacles around the base of the very slender spire. The Sherard coat of arms is above the west doorway and above that is the date of its building. The neighbouring rectory was built at the same time, and, again, it has a dominating feature of a large imitation-Jacobean gable.

The stretch of railway line between Oakham and Melton Mowbray passes south of Saxby and north of Stapleford Park. A glance at the map shows how the contractors building the line in the 19th century finally had to make this

big sweep well away from the park. The 7th Earl of Harborough did everything possible – including having his retainers
do battle with the engineers and surveyors – to prevent the
railway from running anywhere near the park and the result
is still known as 'Lord Harborough's Curve'.

The site of the 'lost' village of *Stapleford* is somewhere in
the park and now, apart from the churchyard cross of the
original medieval church, all that remains are the hall, the
stables, and George Richardson's church which is situated a
short distance from the park entrance. The hall was started
by an early member of the Sherard family but is in the main
of the 17th century and improved at the end of the 19th
century. It is now a country house hotel. St Mary Magdalene
is a more elaborate building than the one at Saxby, and it has
all its original furnishings preserved. Around the outside
walls are 38 coats of arms of the Sherard family and the
families into which they married, and above them are
pinnacles in the Gothic tradition. Inside there is the vast
family pew (with a fireplace) and many Sherard monuments
in the short transepts.

SCALFORD AND CHADWELL

If you approach *Scalford* from Norman Way in Melton
Mowbray, you pass the entrance to the Scalford Hall estate
where there is now a conference centre and a nursing home.
Leaving Melton by Thorpe Road you arrive in the village at
the bend of the horseshoe-shaped Church Street which
virtually wraps itself around the church of St Egelwin the
Martyr. Just to the east of the church is a very active Stilton
cheese creamery and, in a wall between it and the church
there is a well with a plaque: 'Scalford Spout – Restored in
Commemoration of the Queen's Silver Jubilee 1952–1977'.
The two ends of Church Street finish up in King Street,
where, next door to the King's Arms, is the old Primitive
Methodist chapel; closed some 20 years ago, it is at present a
paint store. Originally there were the two chapels but now all
the Methodists worship in the Wesleyan chapel of 1874 at the

corner of New Street and South Street. Back in Church Street, No 31 is the old bakery.

The dedication of the church to St Egelwin the Martyr is unique but there is some doubt as to his actual existence. St Egelwin's has some interesting features; the tower has the typically local arrangement of a quatrefoiled lozenge frieze below the battlements with pinnacles and gargoyles, and the south porch (formerly with an upper storey) has three niches on its face and one on each of the side buttresses. In the churchyard, very near to the south entrance, is the base of a cross. Inside, note the mechanism of the old church clock, understood to be c1735. There is a Saxon stone preserved in the remains of a rood stairway, and the faces of seven medieval worthies appear in effigy on the chancel arch. In the north aisle note the two early 14th century tomb recesses, and also an old wheeled funeral bier.

I have coupled the hamlet of *Chadwell* with Scalford partly because it is in the same group parish but mainly because the whole of little St Mary's church can be dated as built before 1300. Four round pillars, with decorated capitals, remain on the north side indicating that there used to be a north aisle. On the other hand, the arcade to the south aisle has octagonal pillars. Note the unusual piscina and the tub-shaped font.

SEAGRAVE

—— The one-time isolated village of *Seagrave* lies in a valley of the Wolds a mile or so off the Roman Fosse Way (A46 trunk road). The lurid history of the 12th and 13th century Segrave (sic) family, who took their name from their place of origin, can be read in Arthur Mee's *Leicestershire* book.

East of the church the old rectory still stands after rebuilding and, near the Pond Street turning, Abbotsbury Court is dated 1607. The church of All Saints is kept locked but the key is held by the village shop. The church tower is similar to many described in these pages – quatrefoiled lozenge frieze below the battlements – but without the pinnacles of many others in the area.

Inside there is both a north aisle and a south aisle. Between the south aisle and the chancel is an unusually large opening in the wall. Over the chancel arch is an extremely dirty coat of arms: this is presumably too high to look after but more carefully preserved is a case containing two old musical instruments of the early 19th century, a serpent and an ophicleide. On the north wall of the north aisle are large boards displaying The Creed and the Ten Commandments, whilst in the south aisle The Lord's Prayer is actually painted on the wall. Finally, note the circular Norman font with its segmental arches and two old chests – one with three locks and the other with a single lock.

SIBSON, SHEEPY MAGNA AND SHEEPY PARVA

Dick Turpin, the highwayman who is recorded as living nearby during the 1730s (see *Fenny Drayton*) is reputed to have used The Cock Inn at *Sibson* as a regular hiding-place after pursuing his calling on Watling Street. This, of course, all came to an abrupt end when he finally met his fate in York in 1739 but the timber-framed inn on the corner of the A444 has a much longer history than its one-time guest. Originally a tithe barn built c1250, it later became an inn and probably acquired its name because it was a venue for cock-fighting. Near the other end of this tiny village is the 1839 National school building and, more or less central, is the church of St Botolph with thatched Rose Cottage near to the church entrance.

There has been a church here since 1154 but the oldest part of the present building is the chancel of c1300 with much of the rest rebuilt in 1726 after the steeple fell down and, as a pamphlet inside says, took part of the church with it. The chancel was restored in the early part of this century but retains the original triple sedilia. Note the 14th century effigy by the altar where the figure is of a man holding in his hands his heart which he is offering to God. Note also the brass to Thomas Neale who had been rector here for 67 years when he died in 1859, and also the brass to another rector, John Moore, who died in 1532. Outside, the pinnacles on the tower have the look of fat vases.

A mile or two to the west *Sheepy Parva* and *Sheepy Magna* stand on either side of the river Sence with but the one church of All Saints in Magna. Here, at the base of the outside of the west wall of the tower is another 14th century recumbent effigy of a man holding his heart between his hands. There is a very long and detailed guide to this church but it is rather taken up with what was destroyed in the restoration of 1778 and the memorials to a succession of rectors of the Fell family! The 26 pages give you all you need to know but the chief interest here are the four stained glass windows in the south wall – two designed in 1879 by Sir Edward Burne-Jones, founder of the Pre-Raphaelite Brotherhood, and two by C.E. Kempe in 1897. Both men were highly distinguished and respected artists of the late Victorian era.

At *Sheepy Parva* there is an old mill and a mill pond out of the river Sence. At one time in Warwickshire but now, after the redrawing of borders, back in the county, the moated New House Grange stands about half way between Sheepy Magna and Orton-on-the-Hill where there is a medieval timbered tithe barn over 140 feet long.

SLAWSTON, CRANOE, GLOOSTON AND STONTON WYVILLE

—— These small villages are linked together for two reasons. First, in the 15th century the Brudenell family of Stonton Wyville purchased the manor (or the estate as we would call it today) which comprised all these places, and second, they lie in somewhat close proximity to each other in what Hoskins calls beautiful rolling countryside, although each is somewhat secluded.

At one time the most important of the villages on the estate, *Slawston*, to the north-west of Medbourne, is a very quiet place now – with no post office or inn – but when I visited it there was much activity at All Saints church due to restoration. Joseph Goddard, the Leicester architect who was responsible for so much restoration of churches in the county during the 19th century – and, indeed, the building of at least one new one – rebuilt the chancel in 1864 but I was unable to discover the reason for the new work. Note the rustic tracery on the 14th century clerestory.

A mile or so north of the village is Othorpe House – formerly known as Slawston Lodge – and between the road and the house is a well-defined site of a deserted village – shown as such on the Ordnance Survey map and the outlines and folds in the ground are clearly visible. A mile to the west, the church of St Michael, with its 13th century tower, overlooks the tiny village of *Cranoe* which has little of historic interest: its church is on the *Glooston* road and a brief stay here is more rewarding.

The course of an old Roman road – the Via Devana – is shown just south of the village on the OS map, and excavations have proved that it was occupied in Roman times; the site of a Roman villa was found in 1946. Like the others in this cluster a quiet place now with few cottages or farms, but the Old Barn inn stands facing, across a surprisingly wide concourse, Adelphi Row, a long ironstone group of cottages. Just west of the inn is the church of St John the Baptist, another church restored by Joseph Goddard, who apparently left very little of the original! The piscina and the heads on the south doorway are original (c1300); outside there is a bellcote with two openings (but only one bell) very similar to those to be seen in Rutland.

The church at *Stonton Wyville* is unusually dedicated to St Denis. Like St John the Baptist at Glooston it has not only a bellcote but was also restored by Goddard, in 1869. It is here that memorials to the Brudenells can be seen: there is a particularly fine altar tomb in the chancel to Edmund Brudenell who is shown in legal robes together with his wife and children. His infant son, sculptured in swaddling clothes, has his own miniature tomb – as Arthur Mee says, a most pathetic monument.

SNARESTONE, SWEPSTONE AND NEWTON BURGOLAND

——— South-east of the former colliery villages of Measham, Oakthorpe etc and the A42 trunk road, this triangle of villages is linked geographically in the valley of the Mease and, although small, each has something to offer. At *Snarestone* St Bartholomew's church, which stands on the B5002, was completely rebuilt in 1752 and enlarged c1834. In the middle of the village, past the Globe inn, there are two period houses, more or less facing each other; one is c1700 whilst the other is of the later 18th century. There are also three thatched cottages in a line, Primrose Cottage, Clematis Cottage and Front Row Cottage.

To the east the church of St Peter at *Swepstone* has the nave and the aisles of the 14th century although the western tower is probably older. The tower was restored in 1842 by the addition of ashlar cladding, and later in the 19th century the rest of the church was restored. In the north aisle there is an altar tomb of the 14th century decorated with coats of arms and a much mutilated effigy of a woman with a close-fitting cap and a wimple hiding her chin; she has a lion at her feet. On another altar tomb is the alabaster effigy of William Humpfrey who died in 1591 depicted in half-armour, sword by side and his hands joined in prayer: he also has his feet on a lion.

In *Newton Burgoland*, the third point of the triangle, there is a brick Congregational chapel of 1807 down a side street. In the main road there is The Belper Arms which bears the legend 'The Oldest Public House in Leicestershire circa 1290 AD'.

SOMERBY AND PICKWELL

——— One of the approaches to Somerby is from the Melton to Oakham road via the turning – left from Oakham, right from Melton – at a signpost which has 'Leesthorpe' as the first of three names. There is no village here now but you will pass the hall on the way to Somerby; and do spend some time in the little church of All Saints in the small hamlet of *Pickwell* before moving on. I was somewhat surprised to find – in this rather isolated spot – that the church was open and that there was a guide, so just a few additional notes. My first thought was 'where is the pulpit?' and then I saw it somewhat ignominiously tucked away on the floor at the west end of the south aisle!

In the chancel is a piscina and a stepped sedilia and in the east wall of the south aisle a niche containing a statue of the Virgin Mary. The font is Norman which gives a clue to the date of the earliest parts of the church – it and the south porch are believed to be pre-1300. Note the niches on the buttresses on the exterior of the south aisle, also the blocked window on the south wall of the chancel – best seen from the churchyard.

On to *Somerby*, and before arriving at All Saints church, you pass the stone-built Somerby House: note the large ogee-shaped decoration over a first floor window facing the road. The church is another with a guide so take a look at the interesting village first. At the west end is a modern Methodist church with a foundation stone dated '13 Oct 1956'. Down Chapel Lane, however, is what is now a private house but obviously the building which gave its name to the lane. There are other interesting cottages here – The Carriers is dated 1871, Burley rebuilt 1930. Claremont Cottage was originally three cottages and retains an old pump in the garden, and finally Charity House, which was built on the site of an old 'hospital'. In the High Street, opposite the ironstone school of 1876, is a group of old houses, including The Old Forge and another dated 1833 on the gable end. The Cottage has a stone griffin over the doorway. Further down, on the same side, is Toad Hall opposite the Old Brewery inn where they brew their own beer.

The first thing to notice about the ironstone church is that it has a central tower – a rare feature in the county. Note the ogee-headed sedilia (with a bench end poppyhead hidden in one of the sediles), and the late 13th century font, all referred to in the guide. One final point: as at Langham, there is a memorial to the men of the Parachute Regiment who trained locally and who fell at Arnhem in the Second World War.

❧ SPROXTON AND SALTBY

—— A first impression on arrival in *Sproxton* would be that it was a village without a church but the map will show that St Bartholomew's church stands aloof and physically much higher than the houses and farms of the inhabitants – in fact, well on the way to neighbouring Saltby! At the time of my visit a disused Methodist chapel stood in the middle of the village and I was informed that it had been sold to an American group. Since then it has been dismantled and transported lock, stock and barrel to the United States. On the other side of the road is The Crown inn which has an 18th century look about it.

Between this small centre and the church there is an open green with scattered ironstone dwellings or farms on the west side, one dated 1795 and another, near to the Stonesby turning, dated 1785. Opposite is the Gothic-looking village hall and from the still preserved bell it can be seen that it was originally the old school built in 1871; this replaced an earlier one of 1800.

And so back to the church, quite a step if you are walking. The ironstone building is typical of the county with the usual battlemented tower complete with pinnacles and gargoyles but without a frieze. This is one of the few churches I have not been able to get into but, despite reading of the numerous decorated corbels inside, I was more interested in the churchyard, as here is one of the few complete Saxon crosses in the country and certainly the only one in the county. Although the base remained in the churchyard apparently for many years it was used as a footbridge on a path to Saltby and was only rescued sometime in the 19th century.

Continuing north-west along the practically straight road from St Bartholomew's, the tiny village of *Saltby* also has its church right outside but not so extreme as at Sproxton. St

Peter's is a small ironstone church with no aisles, mainly of the 13th century although the chancel is a restoration of 1885. There are two gargoyles on each side of the tower, also pinnacles but, unusually in this area, no battlements. Inside, note the six corbels with grotesque faces on each side of the nave and the mechanism of an old clock by the doorway.

A mile or so to the north-east of the church is a long double mound of earth with a tumulus at each end known as King Lud's Entrenchments. The date is unknown but it is of great antiquity. Clearly shown on the Ordnance map, it is now part of a nature reserve.

SWINFORD, STANFORD-ON-AVON, SHAWELL AND CATTHORPE

—— As these four places are clustered around the M1 and the M6 junction at the most southerly point of the county, and in the same group of parishes, obviously they must be dealt with together even though they are, possibly, a little further apart than some other groupings. Roads seem to run into *Swinford*, the centre of these parishes, from all sides with All Saints church as the focal point. A number of tall period houses more or less in the centre have various points of interest. At the corner of High Street and North Street there is a gable-ended house of 1690, and in North Street the early 19th century Kilworth House. The timber-framed Websters Farm in Lutterworth Road has the date 1718 picked out in blue header bricks, and in Chapel Street the chapel itself is now a private house.

By now a church guide may be available, as I understand one is in preparation, but look out for the following points of interest. The north arcade is of the 13th century with waterleaf capitals on the piers whereas the 14th century south arcade piers are only partly embellished with capitals. The chancel end of the church has been altered or enlarged several times since 1778 but there has been no change since the 1895 polygonal arrangement. There is a Victorian iron lectern and a circular font which is probably the oldest thing in the church: Pevsner says Norman but the WI Village Book suggests Saxon. A coat of arms of George III is at the west end, and after looking at the three hatchments over the tower arch, note the carved bosses in the nave roof and the shields on the eight corbels.

A mile or two to the east is Stanford Hall, built in 1697 for Sir Roger Cave in the park through which the river Avon flows. The hall and Motorcycle Museum in the stables are open to the public (Easter until the end of September) so full details are obtainable there. The few houses comprising *Stanford-on-Avon* and St Nicholas church are actually in Northamptonshire but the church which Arthur Mee describes as 'a medieval wonder on the scale of a cathedral for size and beauty', is in the Swinford group of parishes and should on no account be missed.

At the time of my visit, extensive repair work was being undertaken to restore this imposing church so it was difficult to see everything. However, there is an excellent guide so I will just point out some highlights; the many monuments to the Cave family, the 17 Cave armorial hatchments around the church and the single misericord in the chancel. Finally, the guide draws particular attention to the carved female heads at the top of the pillars supporting the arches.

Going westward along the river Avon from one border outpost to another, *Catthorpe*, the most southerly of all the county villages, we find that, metaphorically, it is boxed in on all four sides: by the M6 and the M1 on the north and east, by Watling Street (A5) on the west and the Avon running more or less along the boundary to the south. The little 14th century church of St Thomas has several interesting features, apart from its modern lychgate, the circular font is 13th century and behind the entrance door, of the same date is a coffin lid with the effigy of a woman holding a heart, engraved in a sunk trefoiled recess. Note also the six corbels in the nave embellished with angels or grotesques.

The fourth parish in this group is *Shawell*, almost midway between the M1 and Watling Street, but if ever a place qualified for the designation 'hidden' this is it. When approaching the village from the north, the corrugated iron Methodist church is the first feature seen; then by going south along a narrow road past the cottages, and an interesting chicken farm, eventually you will see All Saints church standing remotely on a small hill at the most southerly tip of the village. It was locked but apart from the Perpendicular tower the rest is of the mid-Victorian era, rebuilt by William Smith.

I was, however, agreeably surprised to find another of the plaques (see *Drayton, Hallaton, Kings Norton, Medbourne*) to commemorate the Silver Jubilee of Queen Elizabeth II, on a post right by the pathway up to the church. Headed 'The Manor of Shawell' it mentions Peter Temple who was one of the judges at Charles I's trial. He had his estates at Shawell confiscated at the Restoration and died in the Tower in 1663. Alfred, Lord Tennyson, is also mentioned because he often stayed at the old rectory and wrote some of *In Memoriam* here.

SWITHLAND, CROPSTON AND THURCASTON

—— A glance at the Ordnance map will show that it is sensible to unite this triangle of villages. There is a tenuous link in that the Swithland and Cropston reservoirs were both built in the 19th century to supply Leicester with water, and Cropston is a hamlet of the parish of Thurcaston.

When you approach *Swithland* from Rothley Plain and drive under the 'Great Central Steam Experience' railway bridge, you come at once to the southern end of the reservoir where many people cannot resist feeding what must be very overfed ducks and swans! At the entrance to the village there is a granite gazebo, apparently on a wall to a farm and, further down the village street beside the school and practically opposite the Griffin Inn, is another one. They mark the extremities of the site of the old hall which was burnt down in 1822. The school, which is still in use, was built in 1843 and a griffin is inscribed over the date on the wall. Just a little further west is a cottage dated 1842.

The present Swithland Hall, completed in 1852, is situated east of St Leonard's church where, in the churchyard, there are many of the slate tombstones for which Swithland became famous. In the church is a wall monument to Sir John Danvers who was responsible for the south aisle (the date 1727 on the east wall); he was also responsible for removing the cross of c1500 from Mountsorrel to set it up in his own park. From the churchyard it can be seen at the far end of a field south of the church. Also in the churchyard right against the fence, is the tomb of Sir Joseph Danvers who died in 1753. Actually only half the tomb is inside the churchyard with the other half, containing a beloved dog, outside in unconsecrated ground!

On the way to Thurcaston from Swithland, and right in the middle of *Cropston* at the road junction of the B5328 and B5330, you will see the black and white external treatment to what is a fine example of a timber-framed cottage of – or at least parts of it – the late 15th century. In nearby Causeway Lane there is another timber-framed cottage but of two centuries later.

The church at *Thurcaston* is very nearly the most southerly building. On the way there is the Methodist church, a small cottage dated 1824 and further along the same road, near the church, is the 15th century cruck-framed building called Latimer's House. Although Bishop Hugh Latimer was definitely born in the village, and in 1555 burnt at the stake on the orders of Queen Mary Tudor, there is no evidence that this house was his birthplace. Across the road from the church is the old school which still retains its bell: this is now the church hall. In All Saints church there is, of course, a memorial to Thurcaston's most famous son, Bishop Latimer but only erected in 1843. At the back of the church is all that remains of a slate headstone of Elias Travers, a rector who died in 1641; this is believed to be the earliest slate headstone in the county. There are four corbels on each side of the nave embellished with grotesque faces supporting the roof but the most interesting feature here is the rare wooden chancel arch which rests on stone corbels: these two corbels are also embellished with grotesque faces.

—— Hoskins calls both these places 'unprepossessing villages' whilst Brian Bailey writes about the 'miners' houses that line their gloomy streets' but now, with coal mining no longer carried on and with new estates cropping up here and there, it is not all that bad! Furthermore, both villages are old foundations and have their places in Domesday Book. Thringstone was 'Trangesbi' in 1086 and 'Thringeston' as early as 1276 with Whitwick as 'Witewic' in 1086 and 'Whytewyk' by 1327. As you near *Thringstone* on the A512 remnants of the Grace Dieu Priory can still be seen in a field (see the entry for *Belton* and *Osgathorpe*) and then, leaving the main road just before it jinks sharply to the right by the Bull's Head, drive through Thringstone into *Whitwick*. Thringstone's church of St Andrew was only built in 1863; it has no tower but is apsed.

St John the Baptist church at Whitwick is more or less midway between the two places and is a much older establishment, mostly of the early 14th century although much restored in the middle of the 19th century. Of the two fonts here one is circular 14th century and the other a more modern octagonal type. In the crypt below the chancel is a late 14th century tomb bearing the badly preserved effigy of Sir John Talbot; it is about seven feet long, as Sir John apparently was in his lifetime! Also in the village is a Baptist chapel dated 1861 and in Parsonswood Hill, just to the north of St John's, is the Holy Cross Roman Catholic church built in 1904. Nearby are the Crapper Almshouses of 1846.

Return back down Parsonswood Hill, turn left and drive eastwards and you will come to the Mount St Bernard Abbey, indicated by a large sign 'Monastery' just before the entrance – and you may take the drive into the car park. Founded in 1835, the abbey was the first Roman Catholic abbey since the Reformation and it was designed by Augustus Welby Pugin, better known for his work on the rebuilding of the Houses of Parliament after the fire of 1834. You are invited to visit the church although you cannot walk everywhere. Curiously, entry is at the east end and it will be seen that the altar is central. There is a full coloured illustrated book available as well as a little *Brief Historical Sketch*. Outside, note the Calvary built into the rocks. Immediately to the north, between the abbey and the A512, is the Blackbrook reservoir.

TILTON - ON - THE - HILL

—— *Tilton* does, indeed, merit its full title because with *Halstead* it is the highest village in the county with the spire of St Peter's church as 'the dominant feature for miles around'. That phrase is taken from a little pamphlet – on sale in the church – entitled *Historic Village Trail* which highlights all the interesting features and even individual houses in both Tilton and Halstead; for such a small place to have this type of guide must be very nearly unique. For the everyday traveller, anxious to get to Leicester from Oakham or elsewhere, Tilton is passed through in a minute – despite an awkward turning by the church – but, for the curious this guide is a 'must': I hope that it stays in print.

The guide tells it all but I will highlight a few features. Across the road from the church is the Rose and Crown which is dated 1707 although there is evidence of an earlier building here. You can park your car in their car park whilst exploring the village and the church. A few yards down the Oakham road is the old village pump which has been carefully preserved and is situated between two cottages opposite the church. At the south end of the churchyard is the old school; originally built in 1844 it functioned until 1974 when it was replaced by a new one. In the churchyard is the shaft of a medieval cross but Tilton's great treasure is the church itself where – a wealth of riches indeed! – you will find another guide.

On entering the church through the south porch (rebuilt in 1600), you are immediately struck with the lightness of the interior – compared with the semi-darkness met with in so many churches – but you will soon be searching out all

Gargoyles on St Peter's church, Tilton-on-the-Hill.

the grotesque faces on the corbels and the carvings on some of the capitals. In the chancel, all on one level, is a triple ogee-headed sedilia and opposite is the 17th century alabaster monument to Augustin Nichols and his wife together with their 12 children. The church guide gives details of the tombs of the Digby family who lived at Tilton for at least three centuries and suggests that the upper part of the font is the only remaining part of the original 11th century church. Outside there are more grotesque faces on the numerous gargoyles all around the partly crenellated exterior of the church: the little village guide says that 'the observant visitor will note that some are quite obscene'!

TWYCROSS, NORTON-JUXTA-TWYCROSS AND ORTON-ON-THE-HILL

Two of these places are obviously linked by the very name, Orton is linked by minor roads to both and Twycross Zoo is inside the triangle.

Twycross lies across the junction of the A444, linking Warwickshire and Derbyshire, and the B4116 (which becomes the B5002 at Snarestone) so it is not exactly hidden or quiet. The village green in the centre of Twycross stands between the two roads and the village pump is preserved there. Nearby is Twycross House, parts of which are dated 1703. Once a hunting box of Viscount Curzon it is now part of a successful private school which also occupies a number of houses in the village.

Curzon was the family name of Earl Howe and in St James the Greater church there is a hatchment bearing the motto 'Let Curzon Hold what Curzon Held'. There is a north aisle, the arcade piers have no capitals, but no south aisle and the nave and chancel are all in one. In 1840 there was a major restoration involving the south porch, the roofs, a reredos and the addition of the west gallery, on which there is a solid coat of arms. Earl Howe's family pew of c1789 is near the altar; take particular note of the little fireplace!

The church contains one of the great treasures in the county: the east window – presented by Earl Howe during those 1840 restorations. It is claimed to be the oldest stained glass window in England. There is no take-away guide in this church but on sale are full details of the window with the dates of individual panels (ranging from 1140 to 1254), the story of how it came into the possession of Earl Howe and a fine coloured postcard photograph.

Before going on to Norton, a quick eastward visit via the hamlet of Bilstone will bring you to the remains of a gibbet post erected in 1800 on the road between Bilstone and Sibson. Retrace your steps and head for *Norton-Juxta-Twycross*, the parish in which Twycross Zoo is situated. This well-known zoo was the location for the BBC's series *One by One* shown in the eighties. The narrow road leads into the small village, where the public house, the Moores Arms, reminds us that Sir John Moore was born here. He founded the school at nearby Appleby Parva, completed in 1697, and still in use as a primary school. Holy Trinity church has a 14th century tower with a figure in the niche on its west side. Although basically of the 12th century, the rest was rebuilt circa 1841 with the box pews, west gallery, pulpit and reading desk all of that time.

At the inverted apex of the triangle, *Orton-on-the-Hill*, there are genuine 18th century box pews in St Edith's church of 1764 and also a three-decker pulpit, still in place in the middle of the north wall. The remains of a christening pew are in the south-west corner and nearby are the bells, taken down from the tower, and the mechanism of an old clock. The ogee-headed piscina is of the 14th century, as is the effigy of an abbot of Merevale Priory in the north transept (or what could be part of a north aisle now dismantled). In the south aisle there is an incised slab to William Foster who died in 1511, and also a coffin-shaped tomb with a Maltese cross on one end and a miniature effigy of a mounted man in armour on the other.

TWYFORD AND THORPE SATCHVILLE

—— The County Council publish a series of helpful leaflets under the general title *Leicestershire Waymark 2000* showing footpaths that have been improved and waymarked. The one showing a triangular walk between these two villages and Ashby Folville provides the link for us here. Approaching *Twyford* from Burrough-on-the-Hill you will see a sign 'John of Gaunt'. No village here and only one or two houses but a brief stop will enable you to see the 'John of Gaunt Viaduct' down in the valley to the left; all that remains of a dismantled railway, and the map shows that it used to wind to the east of Twyford and to the west of Thorpe. The leaflet has a photograph on the cover.

As you enter the village, the ironstone National school, on the corner of Church Lane, is immediately on your right virtually diagonally facing St Andrew's church across the churchyard more or less in the centre of the village. The school, now a listed building and a private house, has its date of 1845 in Roman numerals. There is, however, another plate added, again in Roman numerals, showing 1980 which was the date of its conversion. Note the heads on the hood mouldings of the two doors – as on many of the church porches in the county. Twyford was 'Tuiuorde' in Domesday Book so even in 1086, or perhaps earlier, there were 'two fords' over the brook and now today there are two bridges. The town bridge of three arches was built in 1775 and, after mid-19th century widening still manages to take today's quite different traffic.

And now back to St Andrew's church, where there is a guide available. The main point of interest is the Norman arcade of c1185 on the north side of the nave. The carving on the middle capital is similar to that on a capital in Oakham Castle and a panel by the door contains photographs and attributes both to the same medieval craftsman. Note also the square 13th century font with a foliated cross on one of the surfaces, and the 'Sick and Poor Box' of 1618.

There used to be a windmill between Twyford and *Thorpe Satchville* but there is nothing to be seen now; however, the legend lives on in some poems by George Riley published in 1896. Entering Thorpe, note the Clock House (with its cupola clock) and the Old Forge together on the right hand side of the road. A short way up the hill, turn down Church Lane which contains partly domestic housing but, at the far end on the right, there is a sign on the wall by a gateway: 'The Hall, The Old Coach House and Clock Cottage'. Through it I saw an archway with a cupola, but also workmen and it looked as if the place was being split up into flats. The little church opposite was locked and looked neglected, but I noted the bellcote on the west end.

WALTHAM-ON-THE-WOLDS

—— Although in the 13th century the village was granted a royal charter to hold a weekly market, this had been discontinued by 1800, though an annual horse and cattle fair was still held until 1921. This interest in horses is reflected in Hall Farm at the north-east end of the village on the main A607 road between Melton Mowbray and Grantham, which has a sign indicating that a race horse trainer operates there. Originally the Waltham Agricultural Hall, erected in 1838, stood on the site but when it was demolished the present building was put up using the stones of the hall. Practically opposite is the Wesleyan chapel of 1843 and then, in the centre, and on opposite sides of the green just by the church, are the two inns the Marquis of Granby and the Royal Horse-shoes. At the end of Mill Lane a tower mill without sails has been preserved but now has a house attached.

Dominating the village is the mainly 13th century church of St Mary Magdalene, with its central tower and 15th century crocketed spire. There is a church guide available – including a short village history – which, unlike some, seems to include everything so I will just stress one or two particular features. Pevsner makes only a very brief mention of 'recumbent angels on the roof' but, as the guide points out, the corbels with grotesque faces and the ten angels in wood between the corbels are important decorations of the nave roof, and another ten angels help to support the roof of the chancel. The octagonal font is Norman with intersected arches over leaf forms and a Latin cross; the chandeliers were put up in the early years of the 18th century. Note that the tower is typical of many in the county with pinnacles, gargoyles and a frieze but there are no battlements.

WOODHOUSE AND WOODHOUSE EAVES

——— The road from Quorn leads into *Woodhouse* past the approach to Beaumanor Hall, and at the southern end of the village is the church, dedicated to St Mary-in-the-Elms. The Herrick family bought the Beaumanor Estate at the end of the 16th century and Beaumanor was the Herrick family seat for over 300 years. Their influence was all powerful in the district and, as the church guide says, 'the history of St Mary-in-the-Elms has been closely linked with the history of Beaumanor'. The present hall, which is private, was built in 1846 by William Perry Herrick but interestingly, the architect was William Railton; the architect of Nelson's column in Trafalgar Square.

Just to the north of the church are four houses endowed by one of the Herrick family – Mary Ann Herrick – in 1856, and across the front is 'Offer unto God Thanksgiving'. The useful church guide gives helpful information not only about the church but also about the Herricks so I need only mention one or two points. The pulpit is the remnant of a three decker oak pulpit given by 'William Heyricke' in 1615. Sir William Herrick was the one who bought the Beaumanor estate and who was the uncle and guardian of Robert Herrick – considered to be one of the greatest English lyric poets. Do not fail to see the stone Beaumont lion on the roof above the north aisle; this lion is a reminder that the Beaumonts built an earlier house at Beaumanor but left the area during the reign of Henry VII – the victor of Bosworth Field.

A mile away to the south-west is *Woodhouse Eaves* where the church was built in 1837 to the design of William Railton, the architect of the present Beaumanor Hall. The church is on rising ground on the Swithland Road with the war memorial on the cliff face and the embattled vicarage nearby. In the village is the octagonal Baptist chapel – originally erected in 1796 but completely rebuilt in 1981 – and the Wesleyan Methodist chapel of 1887 is on the other side of the road. Finally, at the beginning of Maplewell Road there is a row of attractive cottages built of rough stones from the Swithland slate pits.

WYMESWOLD

Sir John Evans, the author of *The Ancient Stone Imple-
ments, Weapons, and Ornaments of Great Britain* (revised 1897) writes 'In the museum of Leicester is a "witch-stone" from Wymeswold, a pebble with a natural hole towards one end,

which has been preserved for many generations in one family, and has had great virtues attached to it. It prevented the entrance of fairies into the dairy; it preserved milk from taint; it kept off diseases, and charmed off warts, and seems to have been valuable alike to man and beast'.

I could not resist including the above, quoted in *Memorials of Old Leicestershire* because it recalls the antiquity of this large village (Wimundeswald in Domesday Book) which once had a weekly market held in an area called The Stockwell. St Mary's church, standing in a commanding position at the corner of the A6006 and The Stockwell, is of special interest because of the restoration work done by the celebrated architect, Augustus Welby Pugin – more famous for his work on the Houses of Parliament after the fire of 1834. The church key can be obtained from the vicarage in The Stockwell.

The Revd Henry Alford, later to become the Dean of Canterbury, took over the parish in 1835 and, as the excellent church history tells us, 'found the church building in a very sorry state' and he it was who commissioned Pugin. The story of the church and a brief biography of the very talented Henry Alford should be still available in the church so I will just mention a few interesting features. Before entering through Pugin's north porch, note the ogee arch over it – as there is also at the 14th century south door and the west doorway at the base of the tower. Inside, the roof of the nave, the font, the stone pulpit, a screen, the pews and a sedilia in the chancel are all by Pugin but bosses of the original roof are displayed on the west wall.

Note also the coloured angel corbels supporting Pugin's roof and, under the tower, a big baroque standing wall-monument to Judge William Leeke who died in 1687: the inscription is in Latin with an English translation. Outside again, the nave and tower are embattled; on the tower are pinnacles and gargoyles at each corner.

There are many houses dating from the 18th or 19th century – bearing witness to earlier prosperity – and in Brook Street, running almost parallel with the main road, quite a variety can be seen. On the connecting link between The Stockwell and Brook Street – called Chapel Bar – is a

Wesleyan chapel of 1845. Tucked away, to the side of it, is presumably the original chapel with a plaque on it 'To the glory of God 1801'.

WYMONDHAM AND EDMONDTHORPE

From whatever direction you approach *Wymondham* its most prominent landmark, the 1814 tower windmill, is seen from afar and, arriving at the village you will find that this is no derelict. On rising ground up Butt Lane – a turning by the Berkeley Arms inn – the windmill was bought by a retired builder and, with a tea room, is open to the public. Back down Butt Lane into the wide Main Street of the village, note the old manor house of c1700 on the opposite corner to the inn and nearly opposite the entrance to Nurses Lane on the other side of the Main Street. To the west, note the old bakery which is now an antiques shop, and then, across the road, the Wesleyan chapel of 1891, the former Three Horseshoes inn (now a private house) and The Old Forge which are all in a row.

On the same side of the road is the short Church Lane and there, after passing the National School room now used as a warehouse and just before the lychgate entrance to the churchyard, is the former 1675 Grammar School. Now roofed with slate but formerly thatched, the building is used by the local snooker club. The lychgate, built to commemorate Queen Victoria's Diamond Jubilee, leads to St Peter's church, which stands between Church Lane and Nurses Lane and has a typical local look about it with a limestone spire on top of a 13th century ironstone tower. The key can be obtained from the cottage – itself probably of the 17th century – next door to the old Grammar School. There is an exceptionally fine guide to the church, complete with drawings and photographs so I will just stress a few features of particular interest even though they may be mentioned in the guide.

In the south transept is an early 14th century cross-legged effigy of Sir John Hamelin, now resting on the incised tomb-chest of Sir Thomas Berkeley who died in 1488. There is also a brass of Dame Margery Berkeley who died in 1521. Note also in the south chancel a squint and, in a glass case, an old musical instrument which used to be played in the church before the installation of the organ. The guide describes carvings on the arcade capitals in detail but note also the grotesque faces on the corbels supporting the nave roof. In the churchyard to the east of the porch is the base of a cross; do not miss the tombstone of one Samuel Pears which is to be found opposite the west wall of the tower.

Edmondthorpe, the rather scattered village just to the south of – and very much linked to – Wymondham, has its own historic church of St Michael which, once again, has a comprehensive guide. Its chief glory is what the *Memorials of Old Leicestershire* calls the 'large and sumptuous monument of alabaster and black marble' of Sir Roger Smith and his two wives against the east wall of the south aisle. At the other end of the south aisle there are two large paintings representing Moses and Aaron, and above these is the hatchment of Charles Pochin who died in 1817 and is buried in Barkby. It was the Pochin family who took over Edmondthorpe Hall in the 19th century and the initials 'W.A.P.' and '1856' are on the preserved old pump outside the 1863 school which is now a social club. The hall is a ruin but the extensive stables and a lodge, both of 1868–69, can be seen from the road. There is another lodge on the Teigh Road inscribed with the date 1867.

HIDDEN
RUTLAND

If you approach Ashwell from Oakham, you pass HM Ashwell Prison on the right just past the Langham turning. On the left are the kennels where the hounds of the Cottesmore Hunt are kept, then further on the right, and partly hidden by trees, is Ashwell Hall which, although it has a Tudor look, was only built in 1879. Past a garage and the village hall, in a little sunken glade is a well, marked on the large scale Ordnance map, which bears the following inscription:

All ye who hither come to drink,
Rest not your thoughts below,
Look at that sacred sign and think
Whence living waters flow.

Unfortunately, 'that sacred sign' was a cross which used to crown the well but is no longer there.

At the beginning of the Cottesmore road is the old rectory beside St Mary's church and a short way past the church the former almshouses at No 5. Further along this road is the Primitive Methodist chapel of 1915, and some houses designed by William Butterfield who was also responsible for the 1851 restoration in the church under the patronage of Viscount Downe.

The church dates back to the 12th century but was, apparently, rebuilt in the 13th century when the north and south chapels were added and, despite the Victorian restoration, its layout has remained much the same, with no clerestory. The great features here are the effigies in the two chapels and an incised slab to John Vernam (died 1481) and his wife. In the south chapel is the rare oak effigy of a knight of c1320, and the Vernam slab, and in the north chapel (now the vestry) is an alabaster effigy of a priest, c1500, reputed to be the Vernams' son.

In the north aisle, almost hidden by the organ, is a late 13th or early 14th century double sedilia with ballflower hood moulds: incidentally, ballflower decoration is much in evidence here both inside and outside, including the porch.

The well, Ashwell.

The sedilia in the chancel probably date from the Victorian restoration but the double piscina, although restored, is of a much earlier date. On the north side of the sanctuary is a large 15th century recess with odd niches and the letter 'T' all over the arch.

Finally, before leaving the churchyard, view the grave, behind the cross, of the Revd James Williams Adams who in 1881 was the first clergyman to be awarded the Victoria Cross and who died here in 1903. A brief story of his life, and the story of his exploits in India which won him the award, are recorded inside the church.

Although the restored tower windmill, just off the A47 trunk road on the way to Barrowden is known as Morcott mill, it acts as a link between the two villages with *Barrowden* being at a lower level in a slight valley on the Northamptonshire border. After passing the windmill and the old school of 1862 (now a private house), you will immediately see the large expanse of green with a rectangular duck pond. Do be vigilant concerning the ducks when going to look at the church, tucked away in the south-west corner just off the green; the villagers are very proud of their ducks!

First, a mention of Thomas Cook, probably Barrowden's most famous son, or rather 'adopted son' because he was born in Melbourne in Derbyshire but, as an itinerant Baptist minister, he spent some time in Barrowden, where he met his wife-to-be; after their marriage they moved to Market Harborough. The beginning of the now world-renowned travel agency stems from the 5th July 1841 when he hired a special train to take some Leicester temperance supporters to a rally at Loughborough. Up Chapel Lane from the green is the Baptist chapel of 1819 (where he would have preached) and on the gate there is a plaque, erected in 1991 to 'Thomas Cook – Train Travel Pioneer – Celebrating 150 Years of Thomas Cook Travel 1841–1991'.

Back past the little post office, with an 1836 cottage opposite, to the green overlooked by the Exeter Arms – a reminder that the village was once owned by the Cecils of Burghley House – head for the duck pond and then go down the little road in the corner which ends with St Peter's church. There are several period cottages on the approach to the church, including one of 1805 and, north of the church, are 17th century Pepperday Cottage and Church Farm which has a barn with arrow slits. The first thing to notice about the church is just how wide it is in comparison to the length, but let the excellent seven-page guide do the work for me. However, do not fail to see the recumbent carved figures supporting the chancel roof and the carved corbels in the nave; the guide explains all the symbolism of these carvings.

Return to the A47 via the windmill, and then, after a short run westward, turn right on to the A6121 and *Morcott* is immediately north of it on either side of the road to Wing. There are a number of 17th and 18th century houses here, including Sundial House (formerly known as the Priest's House) north-east of the church and dated 1627, and the manor house of 1687. In Tyler's Row the Gilson almshouses, founded in 1612, have been modernised and are still administered by a trust. The former Baptist chapel is now the village hall and a former Wesleyan chapel is in private hands, leaving St Mary's church as the only religious building in the village.

St Mary's, with its impressive three-stage tower and short spire, is considered to be the most complete Norman church in Rutland. Outside, note the unusual circular 'pancake' oculus window above a niche which, in turn, is above the west doorway: both doorway and window date from Norman times. Inside, the early 12th century nave is a perfect example of Norman work with the north aisle being added in 1150 and the south aisle c1200. Perhaps the earliest feature is the tower arch with Anglo-Saxon fragments built into it – unfortunately, only visible within the tower. The last pillar of the south arcade supporting the arch has a capital with a carving on it of two snakes – each with its tail in the other's mouth, considered to be a symbol of eternity.

There are other interesting carvings, of rams and human heads, on the capitals on the piers of the north arcade, and in the south aisle is a recess containing the tomb chest and an incised slab referring to William de Overton who died in the 15th century. Finally, note the two hatchments over the tower arch and the fine carving on the Elizabethan pulpit.

Tixover is included here because, like Barrowden and Morcott, the hamlet stands just off the A47 to the east of Barrowden and, although in a joint parish with Duddington (Northants), it is very much a Rutland church not to be missed – standing all alone in a field by the river Welland. Pick up the key from Manor Farm, the last farmhouse in the village, and you can then drive through the fields to St Luke's church. St Luke, incidentally, is the present dedication although, as the guide says, Pevsner and Hoskins both use St Mary Magdalene – probably an earlier dedication. Whatever the name, find the very detailed guide to this remote – but certainly not abandoned – church and, after viewing all of architectural interest here, just enjoy the quietness.

BELTON-IN-RUTLAND

—— My Ordnance map (revised 1986) still shows this village as 'Belton' but, in the centre of the village, on the side of the 17th century Godfrey's House there is a plaque put up in March 1982 to commemorate the renaming of the village by the Duke of Rutland. Thus 'Belton' like 'Braunston', has been differentiated from a place of the same name in Leicestershire and, in this instance, with the same spelling (see *Belton* and *Osgathorpe*).

Belton is the most westerly of the villages of Rutland lying along or just off the A47 and, as at the time of writing the main road was being realigned between the two ends of the 'horseshoe' embracing the village, approach by New Road, the first turning when coming from Leicester. On the left is the Old Rectory with a Tudor-Gothic look but built in 1838–39 and now useful for bed and breakfast. Continue into the centre and opposite Godfrey's House is the early 18th century five-bayed Westbourne House and, on the same side of the road, right by St Peter's church, is The Old Hall which, being of the late 16th century, pre-dates all the other period houses here.

Just past the church, at the junction of Chapel Street and Nether Street, is the war memorial which appears to have been built on the base of an old village cross. The WI Village Book relates that Charles I is believed to have rested on the base after his defeat at the Battle of Naseby: true or not, the stone base is still known as the 'King's Stone'. In Chapel Street is The Old School House and the Baptist chapel itself which is dated 1842.

The guide to St Peter's church is part of *A Guide to the four Churches in the parishes of Uppingham with Ayston, Wardley and*

Belton but details of the church are all included so I will just fill in any gaps. In the chancel there is a fine alabaster slab incised with the effigies of Thomas Haselwood, who died in 1559, and his wife. The Old Hall, where the church key can be obtained, was the Haselwood mansion. Note particularly the drain of the bowl of the piscina in the south aisle; the guide says it has 'a head with protruding tongue and asses' ears' but both Arthur Mee and Pevsner refer to 'a monster'!

Outside again, observe that the lozenge friezes below the battlements on the tower are not all the same, and then search for what must qualify as one of the most hidden 'things' – certainly the most hidden tombstone – in both counties. This 13th century tombstone is on top of the church-yard wall – right by the telegraph pole on the pavement below – and two effigies can be made out. No mention of it in the guide so one wonders just how many people discover it.

BRAUNSTON AND BROOKE

―――― Braunston on the Ordnance Survey map but, to distin-guish it from 'Braunstone', now engulfed by the conurbation of Leicester, the village is correctly called *Braunston-in-Rutland*. The village is full of buildings, manor houses and cottages, built of the local ironstone. The very first encoun-tered when approaching the village from Oakham is the Old Plough public house of uncertain age. Down Church Street, past Gainsborough Cottage and the road to Brooke, you arrive at the manor house – the former home of the Hanburys – with Manor Cottage opposite and, by the river Gwash, the village hall which was built after the First World War as a war memorial. Around the corner is the other inn here, the Blue Ball, opposite All Saints church and, in the corner of the churchyard by one of the gates, Church Cottage which was once a school.

The route has now become Cedar Road leading back to the main road. On the right hand side of a small green is Quaintree House with the cedar trees which give the road its name. Through dating of the roof this manor house appears to be medieval although much of it only dates from the 16th century. Note from the road a building which looks like a chapel. All around or near this little centre of the village are dated houses eg 1803, 1812, 1860 and, right by the little garage, one of 1661 and a former toll house of 1640 – possibly older. Opposite Quaintee House is a former chapel of 1868 now part of the shop and garage complex, and the garage owner told me that the pumps stood where the old forge used to be.

On my visit to All Saints church the guide was apparently out of print, so I will comment on the important features. Much of the church is 13th century although the chancel arch of circa 1150 remains from an original building. The tower and the clerestory date from the early 1400s and here is one of the features for which this church is noted. A primitive crudely carved female stone figure – used for untold generations as a doorstep and only rediscovered early this century during repair work – stands in the churchyard right beside the tower. A pagan relic, Anglo-Saxon or a later medieval carving? No one knows the history.

The other feature of note is the collection of wall paintings on the east wall of the south aisle and, on the south wall a large wheel which E. Clive Rouse has suggested may show part of the Seven Sacraments. Also in the south aisle, at the west end, is a stone coffin; note also the curious stepped base to a window in the north aisle. The vestry is 19th century but the doorway into it from the chancel is Norman. As you leave by the south doorway, note the hood mould with dogtooth decoration of a slightly later date – probably early 13th century.

Barely a mile from Braunston is *Brooke* which, according to Hoskins, is 'one of those remote little places which one instantly feels is a personal discovery to be treasured and visited again and again when anywhere within its aura'. The site of the original, long deserted, medieval village is shown on the larger scale Ordnance map but the present Brooke – not all that remote now – is only a tiny hamlet. The above quotation is taken from the very detailed illustrated guide to

St Peter's church, which is a gem and of the greatest interest because, having been rebuilt in Elizabethan times c1579, it has more or less stayed the same ever since.

The church did not escape completely from Victorian restoration, but the box pews, family pews, pulpit, reading desk, stalls and screens have all been retained. There is a drawing of a medieval wooden chest which was carved from a solid tree trunk; you will find a very similar one in the church at South Luffenham.

Less than a mile on the road back to Oakham is Priory House which is of the late 17th century and stands near the site of a mansion built in the late 16th century after the Dissolution. The mansion was built on the site of the former Augustinian Brooke Priory founded before 1153. In the grounds are the ruined gateway and porter's lodge – not a dovecote as the map and Arthur Mee have labelled it – of that Elizabethan mansion. Earthworks and landscape features of both the earlier establishments can be traced in the immediate vicinity.

CALDECOTT

—— At the bottom of the steep Rockingham Hill leading out of Northamptonshire is a long straight causeway. About half-way along, just after crossing the river Welland, the 'Rutland' sign tells you that you have entered the former county. At the end of the causeway you are certainly made aware of another stretch of water – the Eye Brook – because of traffic lights which control the passage of vehicles over a rather narrow bridge. The Eye Brook, which rises somewhere north of the A47 road near Tilton, flows into the river Welland to the east of Caldecott but on its way it figuratively passes through what is called the Eyebrook Reservoir. A fine view of this can be had from a high point on the road between Caldecott and Uppingham; I mention it because 617 Squadron – the Dam Busters – made one of their last practice runs over it before their historic attack on the Mohne Dam in May 1943 during the Second World War.

The southernmost village of Rutland Caldecott, with its awkward dog-leg corner, is probably in most people's minds somewhere to get out of as quickly as possible. On the other hand if you turn off the main road and stop to have a walk around, there are several interesting features to be seen in the village. The windmill (dismantled in 1909), a 1645 dovecote (destroyed as recently as 1966), along with the railway have all disappeared but at least the village has managed to retain its minute green. On the west side of the green there is an ironstone house with 'WW 1774' over the doorway and next to it is a smaller one with a plaque stating that it was 'Rebuilt 1951'. It may, of course, be of the same age as its neighbour.

There was a Roman settlement at Caldecott and even if those who believe that the church of St John stands on the site of a Roman temple are mistaken, many Roman tiles can be found in the walls. In the porch there is a message: 'Friend, you enter this church, not as a stranger, but as a Guest of God'. Unfortunately it was locked against my entering with no indication as to the whereabouts of the key but Pevsner makes particular mention of the font of c1300 and the 13th century sedilia. Over the entrance to the south porch is a sundial fixed over illustrations of a book and an eye and the inscription 'Your Sunny Hours alone I tell' and the date 1648. Note also the gargoyles on the four corners of the tower.

CLIPSHAM AND STRETTON

The hall and most of the houses in Clipsham, and those of Burley-on-the-Hill, were all built of the local oolitic limestone which had been quarried ever since the 13th century. However, the Clipsham quarry, between the village and Pickworth, closed down in the 1950s but it will always be remembered for one of its last uses – the rebuilding of the House of Commons after it was bombed in 1941. The 18th century hall is not open to the public (although the grounds are open on special days) and the stables, of a much later date, have been split up into flats. The north part of the stables is now a private residence but there is a dovecote attached.

Right by the hall is the largely 12th century St Mary's church; like so many Rutland churches, there is much of interest. Note the unusually shaped Norman font and the much more modern wooden reredos over the altar depicting the Last Supper and other scenes. In the north aisle, over the north door, is a royal coat of arms dated 1603–1648; for many years in the vestry, it was rehung in its present position in 1993. On the floor below is the now disused church clock with its maker's initials and date 'JW 1688' clearly visible. There is an almost identical clock at Nassington but the informative note about the clock tells us 'that it is of interest for its use of a wooden frame – only seen in Midlands districts, about thirty or so are known'.

For the visitor the chief glory of Clipsham is the yew tree drive which is just about a mile eastward from the village and right against the county boundary. Once the main drive to the hall, this extreme example of topiary art, which is now cared for by the Forestry Commission, is open to the public complete with car park and picnic area. The drive stretches for almost three quarters of a mile and ever since 1880 all kinds of birds and beasts (and originally local personalities!) have been shaped out of the lines of yew trees. Over the period of time some of the original shapes have been lost but it is still a magnificent sight.

Return westward to the A1 (the Roman Ermine Street) but before going under it for Thistleton or Oakham, it is worth visiting the little village of *Stretton*, which lies right against it, because of the church – if only one could find out who holds the key! It is of the 12th century but a tympanum over the simple Norman south doorway is believed to be a Saxon coffin lid. The church was saved from complete decay by the efforts of the rector Edward Bradley in the late 19th century, but possibly more people will be interested in the fate of the perhaps more famous Stretton building – The Ram Jam inn on the north side of the A1. Familiar to travellers for centuries, it was virtually destroyed by fire at the end of 1988 but was, happily, subsequently rebuilt.

―――― The name 'Cottesmore' means only one thing to many people who may not even know that there is a village of that name – the Cottesmore Hunt. I have linked it with two other ancient places – all three being listed in the Conqueror's Domesday Book – because today they stand at the points of an invisible triangle around the remains of ironstone quarries and also the very visible (and audible) Tornado Training Base. Little, therefore, is hidden here but there are still points of interest. Visit at the weekend, for except on very special occasions flying only takes place between Monday and Friday!

At the top of the 'triangle' is *Thistleton*, practically on the Lincolnshire border and to the north of the runway. The village takes its name – as Hoskins suggests – from the Anglo-Saxons arriving to find an abandoned Roman village 'where thistles abounded'. There is a sad story behind the rebuilding of St Nicholas church in 1870 by the then rector; this, complete with an apse, was a memorial to his three young children who had all died of scarlet fever. Roman remains have been found in the area, and its entry in Domesday Book shows that there was a settlement here before the Conquest. Note the lane to the west of the village – off the Market Overton road – running northwards alongside the Lincolnshire border through what is called The Thistleton Gap; the large-scale Ordnance map labels it as 'The Drift' and, much more interestingly, 'The Viking Way'.

From Thistleton, the Viking Way can be traced around the north end of the runway only as a footpath, but in *Greetham* the road called Great Lane is shown on the map to be a continuation of it. A first impression of Greetham could be that it is just another narrow village slowing you down whilst driving between Oakham and the Great North Road, but stay awhile and investigate. The village is basically just the main road with ageing stone-built houses on either side, some of them thatched, but virtually in the back-yard of the little post office, and round the corner in Great Lane is the former house of a stone-mason. The building, at one time a slaughter-house, was in the 19th century actually the workshop of the mason who was engaged in restoration work in local churches. He had the habit of removing medieval fragments from the buildings he was working on and incorporating them into the wall of his workshop! The result can easily be seen and photographed.

Some hundred yards or so to the west is Church Lane and at the turning is the old village pump which bears the following legend:

'All ye who hither come to drink
Rest not your thoughts below
Remember Jacob's well and think
Whence living waters flow.'

Across the road and on the other corner is the Victorian old school, now an attractive residence retaining the old school entrance porch and the clock. Note the stream which flows beside the pump, under the road, behind the old school and on behind the houses in the High Street; apparently Church Lane was formerly called Sheepdyke Lane and farmers of old used to dip their sheep there.

St Mary's church is further up Church Lane and although mainly early 14th century – and still with a font of circa 1200 – it was largely rebuilt in the late 19th century, as were so many. Its chief points of interest are twofold: the remains of earlier work including part of a Norman tympanum built into the west wall of the south aisle and oak panelling around the chancel. North-west of the church and beyond the estate of modern houses nearby is the site of a former manor house where Edward I is reputed to have stayed. His wife was the ill-fated and much loved Queen Eleanor, and after her death at Harby in Nottinghamshire he commanded crosses to be erected, including those at Geddington, Hardingstone (Northants) and Waltham Cross in Hertfordshire. These still mark the route which her funeral cortege took in 1290 on its way to London.

Cottesmore, the other point of our imaginary triangle, is a village which, although somewhat overshadowed by the Tornado base, as Arthur Mee says has a history going back

The well, Greetham.

for 5,000 years, but it takes its name from the Old English 'Cott's Moor' and in Domesday Book it is already 'Cotesmore': the modern spelling dates from as long ago as 1237. Except on open days, the base must remain hidden – the guards will have live rounds in their weapons! With housing estates on both sides, let us take a look at the original village which still has trees as in the old pre-war photographs. As at Greetham, but in a wider main street, there are attractive stone-built houses, some of which are thatched and, round the corner from the garage, in Mill Lane, is The Barn. The south wall of this building, which is now a house, is one side of a dovecote with all the nesting boxes in situ – the remaining walls have been destroyed.

St Nicholas church, with its magnificent broach spire of the early 14th century and even earlier Norman zigzag on the doorway, stands in a commanding position in the centre of the village and is to be commended for its useful little guides. I would only suggest that you do not overlook the font of c1200: 'A very strange piece' says Pevsner! Before you leave the churchyard have a look for the grave of Edward Chapman Clayton, who was well known in hunting circles early in the century. It has a gravestone with a large horseshoe carved on it together with the following lines:

'When you lay me to slumber no spot could choose
But would sing to the rhythm of galloping shoes
And under the daisies no grave be so deep
But the hoofs of the horses will sound in my sleep'.

There is nothing tangible to be seen of the Hunt in the village; the Cottesmore hounds moved from Exton to Cottesmore in 1788 and are now kennelled in stables on the Oakham to Ashwell road opposite the prison. Finally, when leaving the village and taking the road to Ashwell, you cannot miss the Rutland Railway museum where, with just three quarters of a mile of track on an old iron-ore siding laid and maintained by volunteers, there is the largest collection of industrial locomotives and freight wagons in the country.

—— *Edith Weston* gets its name from the fact that, in pre-Conquest days, this western area of Rutland belonged to Edith, the wife of Edward the Confessor. It could only have been a settlement then but, whatever the changes over a thousand years, Edith certainly would not recognise it now, especially in high summer when it is more like 'Edith Weston-on-Sea'! With the Rutland Sailing Club to the west of the village, and a large picnic area opening up an approach to the former Normanton church to the east, nothing is hidden here and the proximity of Rutland Water is enjoyed to the full.

The village is attractive with many of the houses being built of local stone, and originally these were grouped around the village green. On the site of the green, in the middle of the village and known as 'Well Cross', are the remains of an old cross. A plaque records that it was resited here to mark the Silver Jubilee of Queen Elizabeth II. Opposite is the old post office. West of the church is the old rectory dated 1626 but that was exchanged in the middle of the 19th century for a farmhouse built c1800 in what is now called Rectory Lane. In its turn this was sold in 1963 and is now a private dwelling called Westona House. At the end of Rectory Lane is the village hall and the rectory is a modern house in Church Lane.

The parish church of St Mary the Virgin has a number of Norman features with the oldest part of the church dating from 1170. As there is an excellent guide available – not only about the church and the village but also about the former St Matthew's church at Normanton – I will just add my own comments to emphasise one or two items. The reading desk is made from four old bench ends, and there are 17th century benches in the chancel with poppyheads. The guide mentions the old turret clock of 1658 and there are photographs of it in the church: the mechanism of the clock is now in the Rutland Museum in Oakham.

There is no village of *Normanton* because in 1764 Sir Gilbert Heathcote depopulated it to allow for the building of his estate and park (see *Empingham*): his mansion was demolished in 1925 and all that remains are the stables – now a hotel – and the former St Matthew's church. The church was deconsecrated when Rutland Water was created, and now, with a raised floor level and with rubble covering all below that level, it has become a Water Museum under the management of the Anglian Water Authority. It is now called Normanton Tower and for a very modest sum, you can learn the whole story of the planning and building of the reservoir: in the guide there is a photograph of the church before the work started on Rutland Water. Sir Gilbert's and other Heathcote memorials, which used to be in St Matthew's, have all been moved to Edith Weston church.

EGLETON AND HAMBLETON

Just to the east of the built-up area of Oakham, along the A606 road to Stamford, there is a turning off to the right. The first part of this road is the remnant of the original A606 before Rutland Water altered the landscape. The signpost indicates that it only leads to these two villages so I will deal with them together. Whereas Hambleton (with two roads from it leading only to the water's edge) stands alone on its peninsula – created by the building of the reservoir – you can drive right through *Egleton*, virtually only a hamlet on the west bank of the reservoir, to the Uppingham road, but stay a while.

Many nature-lovers and bird watchers visit the Rutland Water nature reserve here, best approached from the Uppingham road; note the Old Bakehouse opposite the turning down to the reserve. In the farmyard of Home Farm, off Main Street, there is a dovecote built in 1652, which was being restored at the time of my visit. A few period cottages survive but the great treasure here is the church which also attracts a great number of visitors – although, perhaps, not as many as the reserve!

On the approach to the church is the old Egleton school with the dedication 'Erected by O. Finch Esq. AD 1867' and underneath are two proverbs. You enter St Edmund's church by the south doorway which, according to Hoskins, 'is one of the most photographed church doorways in England'. Over the doorway is a very early Norman arch but within it is a tympanum containing a wheel with spokes supported by a dragon and a lion: some of the work here is believed to be of Saxon origin. I had to use a spotlight to photograph this doorway (which bears comparison with that at Essendine). A leaflet guide is available so I will only add a few notes. The chancel arch has similar decorations to the doorway of c1200 and the font is of the same date. Note the squint which is cut through the chancel arch behind the pulpit. Finally, although the guide mentions that the former north aisle was 'thrown out' in the 14th century, have a look at the outside of the north wall from the churchyard.

Middle and Nether Hambleton are now covered by Rutland Water, whereas the former Upper Hambleton – now only known as *Hambleton* – being on the highest land between here and the Wash, survives on a peninsula jutting out into the reservoir. The church stands more or less on the western edge of the village, and down the hill from it is one important survivor of the flooding of Middle Hambleton. The Old Hall, dating from c1610, stands right on the edge of the water; this attractive building, in private hands, was never a manor house but has been a farmhouse for most of its history.

Back to the village again at the top of the hill there are 1892 estate cottages: the former post office is closed now but a plaque stating 'Hambleton Post and Telegraph Office' and a big clock still face the road. Almost opposite, at the top of the other side of the hill up from the water and just south of the church, is the Priest's House. This is earlier than the Old Hall being dated late 16th century and now it is somewhere you can leave a cat or dog whilst on holiday! Along the village street there is the old vicarage and then Hambleton Hall of 1881 which is now a hotel and restaurant.

According to the church guide Hambleton is 'only one of four Rutland villages recorded in the Domesday Book as possessing churches'. St Andrew's stands on the summit of this little peninsula. The guide describes the church and gives you a little local history, including a mention of the Priest's House above, so I will just add points of interest. In the south aisle there is a coped coffin lid on which, in a recess, are the stone head and praying hands of the deceased with feet sticking out, and a similar coffin lid of a lady is by the tower arch. Note four bench ends with poppyheads and finally the massive iron-bound chest with its three locks.

EMPINGHAM AND WHITWELL

Empingham is the first village travellers meet when visiting Rutland Water from the east – the A606 – either from the Great North Road (the A1 trunk road) or from Stamford across the county boundary in Lincolnshire. Seeing little of it they may not even remember the name. This, however, might have become more widely known as, when the reservoir – claimed to be the largest man-made lake in Europe – was under construction in the 1970s, it was generally referred to as the 'Empingham Reservoir' because of its proximity to the village. Although Anglian Water had voted for that title to be retained when the project was completed, local sentiment wished to keep the name of 'Rutland' alive even though county status had been lost. A massive petition containing over 2,000 signatures finally persuaded the management board to change their minds.

'Rutland Water' it finally became but, even with part of the parish forever under water, Empingham (the 'ham' or 'homestead' of Empa) is still full of interest for those who venture past the White Horse into Main Street. The 13th century church of St Peter towers over the village which can trace a history back to Saxon and Roman times, but until 1924 the Earls of Ancaster at Normanton Park owned most of Empingham. It was the first baronet, Sir Gilbert Heathcote (Heathcote being the family name of the Ancasters) who rebuilt the hall at Normanton but it was his grandson who, c1767, enlarged the park by forcibly 'removing' the inhabitants and rehousing them at Empingham. The hall was

The dovecote, Empingham.

demolished in 1925 although the stables – now a hotel – remain on the Edith Weston road.

There are still a number of thatched cottages to be seen – particularly in Crocket Lane which runs from the church back up to Main Street, where relics of the past domination by the lord of the manor remain: a number of houses there carry – in a stone recess below the roof – the coronet, shield and armorial bearings of the Heathcote, Drummond and Willoughby families, the later Earls of Ancaster. Also in Main Street is Primrose Hall – just in front of Primrose Cottage – which was built in 1860 by the then Earl of Ancaster to house Conservative party meetings, in its time it has been the headquarters of the local British Legion but now is used for storage. It appears to be much older than it is with, strangely, the look of a medieval chapel.

Just to the south of the church is Prebendal House where rents used to be paid before the break-up of the Ancaster Estate. This is not open to the public but can be seen from Crocket Lane, as well as what appears to be one side of a dovecote in the grounds. On the other side of the village, in a field off the Exton Road, is a fine circular stone dovecote with over 700 nesting boxes. At the west end of Crocket Lane, but on the other side of the road to the church, is a house which was obviously once a barn; high up on the west wall, facing Church Street, is a door and an indecipherable date with initials 'W A 16–'.

Before entering what the late W.G. Hoskins called 'one of the finest churches even in this notable little county', take a look at the 17th century Church Bridge which carries the A606 over the river Gwash only a few hundred yards to the south. It was certainly there in 1684 and as late as 1932 was still only 13 feet wide. Its three semicircular arches and massive cutwaters can still be seen from a field to the west of it but recesses for foot-passengers over the cutwaters disappeared at the time the bridge was widened to take modern traffic.

St Peter's church is largely of the 13th century and with its tall 14th century tower dominates the village particularly when seen from a distance. As Hoskins says 'the whole church is worth studying in detail' but, as nearly all Rutland churches deserve this and space does not permit, I can only recommend that, before leaving Empingham, you see for yourself what there is in this fine church. Note particularly the west doorway with its ogee-headed top at the base of the tower, and when inside, after inspecting the architecture do not fail to look at the 13th century triple sedilia and double piscina.

A mile or so along the A606 towards Oakham, you come to the tiny village of *Whitwell* which, you will notice with amusement, is 'Twinned With Paris'. This was done as a joke some ten years ago during a village fete and has remained so ever since – at least at the time of writing. Whitwell is the Rutland Water centre for sailing and wind-surfing but note the little church with its 13th century bellcote; a feature of several Rutland churches and this one is considered to be the oldest. Inside the church is the organ which used to be in the former St Matthew's church at Normanton – now the Reservoir Water Museum.

EXTON

—— Whether you travel to Exton from Oakham by the A606 or from the direction of Stamford, you will need to turn northward at the Barnsdale Lodge hotel and then proceed down the long tree-lined Barnsdale Avenue. Passing on your way the 'Barnsdale' of the BBC gardening programmes, and a small garden centre of the same name, you arrive at one of the two lodges to Exton Park, the home of the Earl of Gainsborough, of the Noel family. Right turn here, follow the road alongside the park, past the other lodge, past the track which leads to the church – sited nearer to the Hall than the village – and you arrive at a large open square which is a fine village green surrounded by trees with the Fox and Hounds on the south side. On the east side of the green is Barham Court which used to be the rectory.

Fort Henry, Exton Park, Exton.

Although more or less surrounded by the park, the village is full of attractive cottages and houses, thatched and otherwise, with those in Pudding Bag Lane being a magnet for artists and photographers! Between the green and this lane is an old well with eight pillars, and nearby the redundant St Mary's school of 1874, still with a bellcote but with the bell removed. Now a private house, it proudly bears a stone over the door which reads 'St Mary's House 1990'. The oldest farmhouse, in Top Street, is dated 1701, and the Exton Park Estate Office in the High Street has the date 1870 over the door.

Near the east end of the park is Fort Henry Lake, named after the Gothic summerhouse of 1785–90 which stands right on the west bank of the lake but it cannot be approached by car without permission. Rights of way for walkers and cyclists, sanctioned by his lordship through the estate office, exist along bridle paths from the village and so this fine 18th century folly can be easily tracked down with the aid of your map.

Return to the village, go back through the green and take the sign-posted track up to St Peter and St Paul church which, apart from one house beside it, stands alone though near to the ruins of the early 17th century hall which was burnt out in 1810. The shell remains fenced off but, both it and the Exton Hall of today, mainly of 1853 but built on an earlier one of 1811, can be glimpsed through the trees from the churchyard. In a field north-west of the church is an octagonal 18th century dovecote; this looks unusual because it had an arcaded cattle shelter added in the 19th century.

The exterior of the church is dominated by the impressive tower, rebuilt c1850 after a lightning strike and topped by little turrets and a spire with its own battlements. Inside is what Adam Nicholson, in a *Sunday Times* article, has called 'the most wonderful sight in Rutland'! The church contains nine important monuments – mainly of the Harrington/Noel/Gainsborough families – and several of them are of outstanding value. Pevsner writes 'There are no churches in Rutland and few in England in which English sculpture from the 16th century to the 18th century can be studied so profitably and enjoyed so much as at Exton.'

There is no guide, and if ever a church needed one it is here, but as I cannot go into great detail a visit to this church is something not to be missed. Actually, the earliest monument does not fit into the time scale in the above quotation; a tomb-chest in the chancel of the 14th century of Nicholas Grene, with an incised cross on the lid and a French inscription. Also in the chancel there is a single 13th century sedile right by one of the monuments. Note that the piers in the north arcade are circular with one of the capitals decorated with heads and foliage and the piers in the south arcade are made up of eight shafts.

Great Casterton, Little Casterton and Tickencote

From time immemorial The Great North Road wound its way through the middle of Stamford in Lincolnshire, into Rutland straight through Great Casterton and back into Lincolnshire a mile or two north of Stretton. Today, however, after modern traffic necessitated the building of a bypass, this very ancient village (and Stamford!) is somewhat more peaceful. What has now become the B1081 (and the main street of the village) is actually part of the old Roman Ermine Street. Casterton – the 'Tun or town by a Roman fort' – was an important staging post on the Roman route northwards from the south to Ancaster. Less than a mile out of the village, along the road to Ryhall and opposite the school, is the site of the thriving Roman town which grew up between the second and fifth centuries. The earthworks, now partly surrounded by the river Gwash, are plainly visible and were investigated by archaeologists in the early 1950s.

At some stage of its development *Great Casterton* was known as 'Brigg or Bridge Casterton' and between the church and the turning for Little Casterton there is the bridge over the river Gwash. Of little interest now, in the 16th century the river was crossed by a stone bridge with three arches and a map of the time showed it as 'Castleford Bridge'. There are some attractive buildings but the main feature of interest is the church of St Peter and St Paul, which is largely of the 13th century although the tower dates only from the 15th century. In the east end of the north aisle are the remains of floral wall paintings; the pulpit, with its sounding board, is 18th century but the rectangular font probably dates from the earlier Norman church of the 12th century which itself replaced a Saxon church. There is a sundial over the entrance, and the south porch, like the rest of the church, is embattled. A few feet from it is an effigy of a priest in an external recess in the south wall: only the feet and the head appear in relief.

Return now for half a mile or so, back over the bridge, to the area known as Toll Bar – a relic of a bygone age when a

The Norman chancel arch, St. Peter's church, Tickencote.

toll was paid here on the old Great North Road – and then take the minor road to *Little Casterton*. A little community on its own now but at the time of Domesday Book it was all one with the rest of Casterton: the 'Major' and 'Minor' only came into use during the 13th century. A lane at the southern end of the single street of mainly unspoilt limestone buildings leads to a house called The Chantry, in front of that a gate leads to the little All Saints church which, with its Rutland bellcote, has a number of interesting features. Unlike many Rutland churches, this is kept locked but there is a little map showing just where the key may be obtained.

The 13th century All Saints retains a lot of an earlier Norman church. Indeed, there is a Norman tympanum which has now been attached to the north wall. This could have been over the previous south doorway but during restoration work in 1908 it was found in use as a windowsill! There is an attractive piscina in the chancel and on the floor is a drain in the form of a four-petalled flower reputed to have come from the demolished church at Pickworth. In the south wall is a recess with two coffin-lids and, though it is (or was) hidden under the chancel carpet, do not miss the 14th century brass to Thomas Burton of Tolethorpe who died in 1381. Another feature which can easily be overlooked is the faint remains of late 13th century wall paintings on the south aisle wall and elsewhere but, more easily seen and in a much better state of preservation are red-lined life-size figures on either side of the lancet window high up on the west wall.

A short distance out of the village is Tolethorpe Hall where a medieval gatehouse remains as an entrance to what was originally an Elizabethan building 'modernized' in 1867. Today, Tolethorpe Hall is best known as the locale of the Rutland Open Air Theatre where the Stamford Shakespeare Company has entertained during the summer months with great success for a number of years.

Tickencote is literally right on top of Great Casterton even though on the west side of the A1. Take the little by-road leading to the village and visit St Peter's church, one of the architectural gems not only of Rutland but of the whole country. The outside of the church is perhaps a little confusing after its restoration in 1792 but inside there is what the little guide calls 'probably the best known feature of any Rutland church' – the magnificent Norman chancel arch. This was untouched during the 18th century restoration; better still, so was the Norman sexpartite vaulted roof in the chancel, considered to be unique. There is a lot to take in here but the little church guide – one of the best I have read – gives you all the answers.

KETTON AND TINWELL

If you approach Ketton along the A6121 from its junction with the A1 trunk road, just inside the Rutland boundary on the extreme western edge of historic Stamford in Lincolnshire, first pause awhile in the little village of *Tinwell*, which has a history reaching back at least as far as Domesday Book and also has strong links with Burghley House ever since Henry VIII, at the Dissolution, gave the church and the manor to the Cecils.

The listed Crown Inn stands on the main road but, immediately opposite, is a little green with the old forge of 1848, its door framed by a large stone horseshoe. At one time this was a post office, as may be seen by the 'VR' letter box still in use, but now the building has reverted to its original purpose – albeit with oxy-acetylene gas to produce ornamental metalwork. In front of this is a well dated 1880, and nearby to the south is what was, until the sixties, the village school and then, until a new one was opened in 1993, the village hall.

Only yards away right in the centre of the village is All Saints church, distinguished by its rare saddleback roof of c1350 which is the only one in Rutland. There is a good eight-page guide so just a few additional comments. There is a brass chandelier of 1730 and note the hinge on the tower door. The guide mentions the monument to Elizabeth (who died in 1611), the sister of William Cecil, the 1st Lord Burghley, but note the unusual way in which her name is displayed. There are less elaborate memorial slabs to other members of the Cecil family but read the sad obituaries in the sanctuary to the two Arnold brothers: the memorial slabs were put up by their proud father who was rector here for 56 years.

Down the road to *Ketton* but, before you reach the village, you pass the least hidden group of buildings in Rutland, the Castle Cement Works which, since 1928, has carried on the tradition of Ketton limestone quarried since Roman times.

The village itself is attractive with many of the houses built of the local stone and St Mary the Virgin church is, according to Hoskins, 'almost incomparable in England for the sheer suave beauty of the tower and spire'. First, the village; in the centre is a well by the Queen Victoria Jubilee Pump with dates 1837–1887, now known as the Fountain. Nearby, at the top end of Redmiles Lane, is a house dated 1699.

Another interesting house is on the corner of the main road and the Empingham Road, opposite to the turning down to the church. It was built in 1890 by the Hibbins family who were local masons for generations and the building is covered with gargoyles and other extraordinary displays of masonic skills. A short distance up the Empingham Road is the shell of a tower windmill without sails.

Beyond the church is a 17th century bridge over the river Chater which has three cutwaters and three pointed arches. Returning from the bridge you will notice several attractive houses, and The Priory – never an actual priory but a prebendal manor house – is immediately opposite St Mary's, and virtually in the churchyard is a listed stone house. And so into the large and imposing church which, despite its location, is strangely enough built of Barnack stone! This church is much visited and so, as there is always a guide pamphlet indicating the points of interest, I can only humbly repeat what it says on an earlier guide, 'Welcome to this house of prayer' and marvel at the glories of this place. On leaving, do not miss the gravestone, nearer the lychgate, of William Hibbins, one of the family mentioned above: it is covered with carvings of eleven tools of the mason's trade.

LANGHAM, BARLEYTHORPE AND BURLEY-ON-THE-HILL

Just two miles north of Oakham and situated mainly to the east of the road to Melton Mowbray *Langham* is on record as being in existence, and with the present day spelling, as early as the year 1202. Today it mainly comprises the compact 'middle' part of the village through which the Dyke brook flows, with the 13th century church and the chimney of Ruddles brewery dominating the skyline as one approaches from any direction. On both the east and west sides, modern housing estates have been built on what were for centuries farmland or orchards.

The church lies between Well Street and Church Street, where most of the oldest houses are to be found, so let us start at the old well-pump near the main road and be surprised that it still pumps water. No 22 is the old forge, with a date stone of 1832 and a number of horseshoes on the wall. No 26 is 1826 and No 30, possibly of the same date, is the only thatched cottage in Well Street. At the main road end of Church Street, running almost parallel with Well Street, some thatched stone buildings can be seen, and then Church Street, which is the core road right through the village, continues past No. 10, an early 18th-century building – until the end of 1995 an inn called The Black Horse – and then Langham House, a one-time hunting box but now a private nursing home.

On the corner next to the nursing home is the Noel Arms. Continuing across Bridge Street, there is the small 1854 Baptist chapel with a little pinnacle on each corner of its frontage and quite a large churchyard. Next the little sub post office-cum-shop – no longer four shops as in the WI Village Book – and opposite is the village hall built in 1890. On the outside wall is a plaque, with a Rutland horseshoe between the dates commemorating the centenary of the Langham parish councils 1894–1994.

Although it has a wing of 1926 and a little clock tower facing Church Street, the old hall of 1665 stands behind in its own grounds and then, immediately after where Well Street joins with Church Street, is the Manor, another 17th century building. Apart from the church, the hall and the Manor appear to be the oldest buildings but some of the cottages in the area may have earlier foundations. The Old Vicarage, on the other side of Church Street, is dated 1790. Next to the Noel Arms in Bridge Street, and facing the main road, is the Old School. Note the stone creatures (sheep? deer?) over the two former schoolroom windows. Do not be misled by the level crossing gates etc between the back of the Old School and the public house car park; the present occupant is a collector of railway memorabilia! A short way along the main road, past the back entrance of the nursing home, is a house called The Gardener's Cottage, dated 1822.

St Peter and St Paul's church, with its massive 13th century tower topped by a 14th century broach spire, is particularly large for the size of the village, but it is a church which Simon de Langham, born here in 1310, would have known. He, as the church guide says, is 'The most remarkable native of Langham', who, after being Chancellor of England, became Archbishop of Canterbury in 1366. He died in France in 1376 and his final resting-place is Westminster Abbey. The full story of Simon's life, together with details of the church plus some history of the church schools, are all in the rather closely printed guide so I will just add a few extra notes concerning this church which I attend.

The guide mentions the ballflower decoration on the south side but a frieze of ballflower and faces continues all around the chancel and then, after a gap, decoration of faces or foliage continues from the blocked north door – with another break on the sides of the tower – right round to the porch again. Unlike many local churches there are no gargoyles on the tower, but good examples of these appear on both sides of the exterior of the nave above the clerestory and under the battlements. The whole of the church is battlemented. Inside, note the arrangement of two windows over the chancel arch which is an unusual addition to the clerestory, the 14th century corbels with faces in the transept and the faces between the arches of the arcades. Finally the memorial plaque to the men of the Parachute Regiment who trained locally and fell at Arnhem in the Second World War is duplicated in Somerby church in Leicestershire.

On the west side of the A606 is Ranksborough Hall leisure centre, a caravan and camping site. A mile southward towards Oakham is the hamlet of *Barleythorpe* which is in the parish of Langham. Here is Barley Thorpe Hall (written as two words above the entrance), now a residential home for older people. The hall was acquired by the 5th Earl of Lonsdale towards the end of the 19th century and was owned by him until 1944. He was, at different times, master of both the Quorn Hunt and the Cottesmore Hunt but his name will be preserved for posterity by his gift of the Lonsdale Belt.

Due east of Langham, across both the railway line and the Ashwell road and about a mile further along is the great baroque mansion of *Burley-on-the-Hill* built between 1694 and 1708. At the time of writing the house and estate buildings were being restored and converted into flats and cottages. Holy Cross church, right by the house and connected to it by a corridor, is now redundant and in the care of the Churches Conservation Trust. On the green in the little hamlet of Burley is an old smithy which has recently been renovated. It is reputedly the building which inspired Longfellow's poem which begins 'Under the spreading chestnut tree the village smithy stands'.

LYDDINGTON, STOKE DRY AND SEATON

—— *Lyddington* is a most attractive village some two or so miles from Uppingham, and has become well known because of its famous Bede House, part of a manor house belonging formerly to the Bishops of Lincoln which was converted into an almshouse in 1602, and now administered by English Heritage. An octagonal turreted watch tower in the main street indicates the approach to where it stands right beside the church, and it is normally open between the end of March and the end of September with the usual excellent English Heritage historical guide.

As St Andrew's church is so near, and the west entrance of the church almost adjacent to the Bede House entrance, it makes sense to visit the church before looking at the mainly ironstone village. The dates of various parts of this lofty building can be linked to different bishops in medieval times but a very detailed guide points out all that is important, although I must draw attention to two most unusual features. First, the altar, some distance away from the east wall, is railed on all four sides, and the initials of John Williams, Bishop of Lincoln, who ordered this arrangement, and those of Richard Rudd (R.R.) the incumbent who carried it out, are carved on the rails which are dated 1635. Second, still in the chancel, note the recesses (six each side) for acoustic jars

The watch tower, Lyddington.

which were intended to improve the acoustics in the chancel when the priest was near the altar.

There is just one further feature to be noted here. The guide, in the section about the nave, mentions 'the whole collection of gargoyles [I would call them 'grotesques'] which peer out from the arch pillars' but it was printed before the new additions of 1991. Both are in line with the medieval collection on either side, with the features of Bill Westwood, the former Bishop of Peterborough, sculpted on the gargoyle on the south side behind the pulpit, whilst the one on the north side behind the lectern depicts the legendary Green Man. These two new additions were dedicated by Bishop Westwood himself in December 1991.

Returning to the main street with its wealth of period houses, first look across the street from the watch tower and there is the Priest's House with a stone in the wall inscribed 'R.R. 1626' the date Richard Rudd lived there. South of this is No 17, the Bay House, dated 1656, built of the ochre-coloured ironstone like so many of the older houses here. Retracing your steps in the other direction, note that No 41 has 1814 above the door but a large buttress has 1767 on it. Three doors away is No 47, Pageant House with the Manor House opposite. Immediately after these 17th or 18th century houses is the village green with the base and stump of a 15th century cross, and on the west side of the green is the Old White Hart inn – one of only two remaining in the village.

Before continuing up the street on the north side, opposite on the south side is Swan House, dated 1674, called by Pevsner 'the best house'. Note the tall mullioned windows together with a continuous string course. Next door but one is The Bakehouse and joined to that is The Maltings dated 1765, so The Bakehouse is probably of the same date. Back on the north side again, Lyndon House is followed by No 57 which is the Old Reading Room and No 63 has its date of 1763 recorded but only in Roman numerals MDCCLXIII. I must mention the almost unbelievable recovery story of the only other inn, the Marquess of Exeter, situated towards the north end of the village. In May 1994 the local paper carried banner headlines stating 'Historic Pub Destroyed in Early

Morning Blaze' plus 'just a shell left' and 'the future of the historic listed building remains uncertain'. However, just over a year later, the 15th century inn had been rebuilt, complete with a thatched roof, without losing any of its attractiveness and period charm.

Leaving the village westward and crossing the A6003 after about a mile, Stoke Road leads you to the tiny hamlet of *Stoke Dry*, midway between the main road and the Eyebrook Reservoir (see *Caldecott*). St Andrew's church dates back to the 12th century and is noted for the carved Norman figures on the chancel arch, the Digby Chapel and its memorials of the Digby family and for its wealth of well-preserved wall paintings – particularly that of the Martyrdom of St Edmund. There is a fully comprehensive eight page guide here but I would just draw attention to the oak 15th century screen and outside to a scratch dial on a buttress on the south wall. Immediately south of the church is the old rectory of 1840– 41: it is now divided into two private houses.

On the east side of Lyddington is the village of *Seaton*. The most striking point of interest locally is the Seaton Viaduct of brick, with its 83 arches, built between 1876 and 1878. It is more than three-quarters of a mile long and does, actually finish well past Harringworth in Northamptonshire. The line is still there and, on occasion, still used. Between the viaduct and the village note what is left of the old station where the old rusty bridge has been retained over the now non-existent line. In the village All Hallows church has a late Norman inner doorway and here again the 12th century chancel arch is notable because of the splendidly carved capitals. To counteract this, in what has been described as 'an act of extraordinary vandalism', an old font has been chopped up and converted into a seat placed at the west end of the south aisle.

MANTON AND LYNDON

In Tudor times *Manton* was on a main route from London to Richmond but now it lies just off the A6003 between Oakham and Uppingham at the start of the minor road which runs along the south of Rutland Water. The village is on quite high ground actually overlooking Manton Bay at the west end of the reservoir, and the railway line, linking Stamford and Oakham, goes through a tunnel, completed in 1878, which was driven under the village. You will see on the Ordnance map – just to the west of the Manton turn from the A6003 – the earthworks of the deserted village of 'Martinsthorpe' around what was the stable of the now demolished hall; a public footpath leads up to the site of this medieval village.

After turning off the A6003, take the first left turn and then sharp right at the Horse and Jockey into St Mary's Road; at the east end there is a long two-storey fronted house with a rebuilt gable end dated 1733. South of St Mary's church is a building called the Priory which gives its name to Priory Road, on the northern edge of the village, where there are two bungalow almshouses. Opened in 1981 these replaced the original cottages bequeathed in his will by Thomas Fryer in 1903. The road through the middle of the village, where the church stands, is Stocks Hill and just south of the end of St Mary's Road is the Old Hall which has a date of 1688 at the back but an 18th century façade. Opposite is the forge of 1582.

In St Mary's church there is a very useful guide which also contains a potted history of the village so just a few additional comments. The ironstone double bell-cote at the west end is of the 13th century – one of a number in Rutland – note the very narrow lancet window. The two original corbels used in the rebuilt chancel have the usual medieval grotesque faces on them. There appears to be some confusion over the date of the painted royal coat of arms over the chancel arch. The guide suggests 1796 but *Churches of Rutland* puts them as 'of 1765', five years after the accession of George III to the throne.

Lying a little south of the road from Manton to Edith Weston, the little village of *Lyndon* is somewhat secluded but it boasts not one but two halls, with Lyndon Hall, built between 1671 and 1673, together with its stable block, being immediately adjacent to St Martin's church and accessible through an archway from the churchyard. This church, the only one in Rutland dedicated to St Martin, dates back to either late 13th century or early 14th century and the remains of five steps to the former rood loft can still be seen. There are two treasures here: a Norman font, with crude animal designs, which was dug up in the churchyard during restoration work in 1866, and the remains of an ancient cross are also preserved. Outside, note the scratch dial on the jamb of the south doorway, and the unusually large gargoyles – two on each side – on the exterior of the nave roof.

MARKET OVERTON AND TEIGH

An old Roman stile built into the northern boundary wall of St Peter and St Paul church, gives a clue to the antiquity of Market Overton and, indeed, the church is reputedly built inside the earthworks of a Roman camp. The village was recorded just as 'Overtune' in Domesday Book but the full name in use today was first recorded in 1200 so a market must have been held regularly before that date. The market itself died out in medieval times but many archaeological finds, unearthed during the heyday of the old ironstone quarries which were worked out by 1973, have proved that the area between the village and Thistleton was the site of an Anglo-Saxon settlement which itself was built on an earlier Roman one.

Coins and ornaments – from Roman, Saxon and even pre-Roman times – are now in museums but in the church the tower arch is of the 10th century, the remains of an earlier Anglo-Saxon church and the only work of this date in Rutland. Note also the odd-looking font which dates from the 13th century – it appears to be made up of two capitals. At the east end of the south aisle is a cross from the First World War and on the outside wall of the tower are the remains of a sundial said to have been given by Sir Isaac Newton whose mother came from the village.

The manor house, which was rebuilt in 1866, stands in the

centre of the attractive, largely unspoilt, village and the garden summer house can be seen from the green. On the wall is a sculptured head of Sir Isaac Newton, and on the green stand the stocks – last used in 1838 – and the old whipping post.

Take the road from the church a mile or so to the south-west and you drop down from hilly Market Overton to *Teigh* (pronounced as in 'Tea') – a tiny hamlet with a most unusual church. The ironstone tower is 13th century but the church was completely rebuilt in 1782 and its attractive features have been retained, virtually unchanged, to this day. The pews are arranged facing each other and rising in tiers 'as in a college or cathedral choir' (Pevsner). There is a mahogany font which is placed on the altar rail for christenings, but strangest of all is the west wall. In the middle of this, above the entrance door, is a little pulpit flanked by two reading desks at a lower level. Behind the whole of this assembly is what appears to be a window through which trees outside can be seen. The window is, in fact, only painted on the wall but really does look quite realistic!

NORTH LUFFENHAM AND SOUTH LUFFENHAM

—— When driving to *North Luffenham* from Edith Weston leaving Rutland Water behind you, the road runs past the retired Meteor Jet and a rocket at the entrance of the still active aerodrome (arguably it should have been called Edith Weston Aerodrome!) and then below its western edge until a right fork down Pinfold Lane brings you to the Fox and Hounds, one of two public houses here. Pinfold Lane goes on to Lyndon and along it, before the village boundary is reached, is Manor Farm dated 1640 with a gazebo in the garden and opposite is 18th century Luffenham Court. A turning off this lane is Glebe Road, the road to Morcott, and along here is a house built by Charles Voysey in 1901. Now called Pasture House, it was originally The Pastures and is of great interest to students of this century's architecture, with Pevsner giving it half a page!

In Church Street a number of interesting buildings present themselves, including Home Farm, a former dovecote turned into a house and, just past the little road to the church and the school, a massive octagonal gazebo above the wall of the hall. The school stands on part of the site of the former Luffenham House (demolished 1806) and there is a curved ha-ha at the end of the playing-field – just west of the church. At the east end of Church Street is the Horse and Panniers inn and, after turning into Chapel Lane, the Methodist church and Sundial Cottage of 1647. Diagonally opposite Sundial Cottage, a 17th century archway leads into North Luffenham Hall – parts of which date from the 16th century – and here is a timber-framed barn dated 1555: unfortunately, this cannot be seen from the road.

St John the Baptist church is mainly of the 13th and 14th centuries with a clerestory of the 15th century. The nave roof, of much the same time, is supported by carved oak angels, with at least one of them playing pipes. There are paintings on the south arcade arches, an Elizabethan pulpit and, in the chancel, what Pevsner calls 'the finest piece of display in the church', a 15th century sedilia with the striking originality of the window tracery here. It is double-seated under elaborate ogee arches but positioned in front of an earlier recess. On the wall of this recess is a memorial to Archdeacon Johnson, the founder of both Oakham and Uppingham schools, who died in 1625.

South Luffenham lies a mile or so to the south of its northerly namesake, the road having taken you under the Stamford to Oakham railway line. There is also a dismantled line here – apparently the first railway junction in Rutland was built here in 1850 and this necessitated new building: it is, however, the church and the older part of the village which concern us most. In The Street is the 1847 Old School House which has a gothic look about it and diagonally opposite is the school built in 1877: both are now private houses and the local children all go to North Luffenham. Nearby is the Boot and Shoe inn, one of two public houses in the village, and further up The Street is Tithe House, once a tithe barn, right by the entrance to the church. South of the church is the 17th century South Luffenham Hall, famed for its gardens.

The church has a multi-crocketed spire of the 14th century but it is possibly an older church than its northern neighbour with a north aisle being added in 1190 to the original aisleless fabric. There are the remains of a 15th century screen still in position under the chancel arch of c1300, and the octagonal font is even older. In the chancel is a 14th century mutilated tomb-chest with an effigy resting his head on a pillow; he is unnamed but the tomb bears the Culpepper arms. The capitals on the north arcade are decorated with rams' heads and foliage, whereas the south arcade capitals have only nailhead decoration or none at all. At the back of the church is a seat made out of bench ends, and a three-locks chest hewn out of a tree trunk stands at the west end of the north aisle (see *Brooke*). On returning outside, look up and see the medieval cross on the gable of the 14th century porch and, above its buttress, a scratch dial.

PICKWORTH

Pickworth, which lies almost midway between Essendine and Clipsham near the Lincolnshire border, is only a tiny hamlet – the last remnants of a village reputedly destroyed after a battle fought hereabouts in 1470 during The Wars of the Roses. It cannot easily be linked with neighbouring villages but deserves its solo entry.

There is a 'new' church here which was built in 1821 but, nearby in the grounds of a farmhouse now named Clare Cottage, is the 14th century arch with carved capitals which, standing alone, is all that remains of the old medieval church. It is said that the 'Northamptonshire' poet John Clare, when working as a lime-burner here, used to sit under the arch and so get inspiration for his poetry. He first met Martha, his wife-to-be, in 1817 when she was living at Walkherd Lodge some two miles away: she is immortalized in one of his poems as 'Sweet Patty of the Vale'. The farm, now called

Arch of old church, Pickworth (where John Clare is said to have sat and written poetry).

Walk Farm, is still extant and lies between Pickworth and Little Casterton.

RIDLINGTON AND PRESTON

These two villages, linked together by an unclassified road which peters out past Park Farm, are often bracketed together and are two parishes with the same rector. They are, however, quite differently situated – with Preston, although saved from the through traffic, suffering the noise of the A6003 Oakham–Uppingham road, whereas Ridlington, on a ridge overlooking the Chater Valley, has even now, the same idyllic look Arthur Mee wrote of in 1937: 'This village of golden-tinted stone, where houses are roofed with thatch and tiles, and grassy banks lend charm to the roads...' This was, of course, pre-Second World War when cars were few but there are still six thatched houses in *Ridlington* and the grassy banks still remain; they are well maintained with the old village pump standing on the green in the middle of the village.

The pump in Main Street stands outside Jotry Cottage – quite a large building which bears the date 1787. Almost opposite is the old village school which has a quatrefoil window and is dated AD 1878. This is now the village hall. A few hundred yards to the west is the 17th century Manor House which was once the home of Sir James Harington, reputedly involved in the Gunpowder Plot. Across the road again near Jotry Cottage is Chimney Cottage dated 1771. In Church Lane is another cottage dated 1708. Further down Main Street and past the church is the old post office, no longer functioning, and there is no public house or shop.

The church of St Mary and St Andrew has a surprise or two for the visitor but the chief treasure is a Norman tympanum in the west wall of the south aisle over the vestry door which is not in its original position but indicates the early 13th century origins of the church. The chancel was rebuilt during severe restoration in the 19th century but still surviving is a monument to Sir James, who died in 1613, and his wife; and a plaque opposite reads 'Here under the Communion table lyeth interr'd the body of Edward Cheselden, Gent'. In the south aisle are two more Cheselden monuments and, at the back of the church, on the west wall there is a case containing a number of musical instruments left by Mr John Scott who lived in Ridlington for over 50 years in the 19th century. What about the surprises? There are five misericords in the chancel, quite plain, unlike the elaborated carved types to be found in the great cathedrals but definitely providing support for the occupant of the seat during long periods of standing. Finally, there is a gap indicating where a rood loft used to be and in the north aisle, the remains of steps up to it.

At *Preston*, with the main road diverted away from its original route straight through what is now Main Street, we can look at leisure at some of the stone-built houses; these are mostly of local ironstone and some are thatched. In the narrow street linking the main road with Main Street, more or less in the middle of the village, is the gabled 17th century Manor Farm; next door is the former Congregational chapel which was built in 1830 and on No 29 is a sundial.

St Peter and St Paul's church, which contains work of every period from c1150 onwards, is on the western edge of the village and there is another sundial over the low porch. The chancel was remodelled in about 1320; note the fine ogee-headed single sedile and aumbry in the north wall. As at Ridlington a partly blocked doorway south of the chancel arch is evidence of a rood loft, and the priest's door is richly decorated. Other details about this little church can be found in the guide sheet.

RYHALL, ESSENDINE AND BELMESTHORPE

—— *Ryhall* has grown much in size since the Second World War but the village is very old and mentioned in Domesday Book as 'Riehale' with an entry 'Countess Judith. 2 mills'. The name derives from the Old English 'Halh – a nook, a corner of land or a water-meadow – where rye was grown' and certainly Ryhall has suffered a lot from the river Gwash which from the map appears to encircle the village. Old photographs certainly show much flooding in the early years of the century. At the end of the raised causeway leading from the centre of the village to Foundry Road is one of two old bridges over the river in the village; this one is of the 17th century and is the older of the two.

The centre of the village is The Square – probably in bygone days the village green but now asphalted over – overlooked by the Green Dragon inn which has a 13th century vaulted cellar. Pevsner tells us that this indicates that the inn was built on the site of an old manor house and that there is more evidence in the masonry. The old village pump, from which villagers use to draw their drinking water, still stands in the inn yard. Note the tree in the middle of The Square. The sycamore tree which stands there now replaces an earlier maple tree and a plaque beside it tells the story: 'This sycamore tree commemorates the 80th birthday of H.M. Queen Elizabeth the Queen Mother 4th August 1980. Replacing an earlier tree planted here to mark the coronation of Queen Victoria in 1837'.

As you leave The Square via Church Street to look at St John the Evangelist church, note the little alley Weasel's End with the inscription and date on the wall of the house 'IH 1773'. Before entering the churchyard, go to the end of Church Street and just round the corner from the village hall – originally the village school which was built in 1837 – you will see a dovecote in a corner of the grounds of The Hall. To the north of the church and close to the Green Dragon, there is a house where an attempt at conversion from another dovecote went disastrously wrong; at the time of writing it was unsafe and empty.

When you approach the 13th century porch of the church, before entering by the equally old wooden door note the little stairway which would have led to an upper storey – a priest's chamber and at one time a school. Of particular note in the church is the 'spectacular' double sedilia of circa 1330–40 with stepped seats and ogee arches: the font is of the same period. At the other end of the church, on the west wall, there is a squint; this has been glazed over and through it the churchyard is visible but originally there was a room built on to the church – and there are still remains of a hermitage stemming from the cult of St Tibba, the patron saint of falconers, whose body was transferred from here to Peterborough in the 9th century. As you leave the church, look to the right of the porch and you will see a stone clock face set into the ground (about where this room would have stood) with all the twelve numbers visible. About this, however, I have no information whatsoever!

Return to Foundry Road over the river bridge, turn right

and follow the road through to the hamlet of *Belmesthorpe* where, at the east end and right by the roadside, there is a rectangular dovecote complete with its cupola. It is no longer a home for doves – although the nesting boxes can be seen clearly through the open south wall. The farmer told me that a pair of owls had taken up residence there. Opposite a house called The Granary (dated 1881) is an orchard and behind that is another former dovecote – more successfully converted than the one at Ryhall.

Retrace your steps along Foundry Road to the A6121 and in a mile or so is *Essendine* where the main railway line from Kings Cross to Edinburgh daily carries many thundering express trains under the road. It was not far north of here that in 1938 the LNER 'Mallard' broke the record for a steam locomotive at 126 mph, but it is not the railway which interests us here. The little church of St Mary with its Rutland bellcote is almost within sight of the Lincolnshire border and is reputed to be the chapel of the completely disappeared castle behind it; the Ordnance map shows 'Manorial Earthworks'. The most remarkable survival here is the 12th century doorway with its Norman arch, carved doorposts and a tympanum thought to be of an earlier age. There are more carvings on the inside door posts. Do not miss the quatrefoil low-side window in the chancel wall – better seen from outside.

Just south of the church is another 17th century bridge, this time over the West Glen river – and, like the bridge at Ryhall, it has three arches and cutwaters.

WHISSENDINE

—— Lying a short distance north of the A606 road between Oakham and Melton Mowbray, the long and rather straggly village of Whissendine has two tall features which seemingly mark each end of it: the disused seven-storey tower windmill at the west end and the imposing tower of St Andrew's church more or less at the east end. Just a few minutes walk round from the windmill – and at the start of the Stapleford Road – is Harborough Cottage, originally the home of Lord Harborough's mistress in the grounds of Stapleford Park, and rebuilt here on a smaller scale in 1859; it only acquired its present name in 1919. The Whissendine brook flows through at roughly the midway point of the village and the White Lion inn is right by the road bridge over it and the Three Horseshoes is nearby.

Further east opposite the church and on the corner of Foxhill, is thatched Honeysuckle Cottage which has a small dovecote built into the roof of its modern garage. The white doves find many convenient perches on the church. Past the Foxhill turning, and on the same side, is the Primitive Methodist chapel of 1868 and opposite, hidden by trees, the old manor house.

The large St Andrew's church, to me, has the look of many Somerset and even some Suffolk churches. As there is *A Short History Guide* available, I will just add a few comments. The church, excluding the transepts, is embattled all round and there are many gargoyles and decorations. Inside, note the twelve (six each side) seated figures on the roof corbels in the nave. The guide gives the background to the screen between the south transept, in which there is a piscina with an ogee arch, and the south aisle; the transepts open out into the chancel rather than the nave as is usual. Finally, note the coat of arms over the locked north doorway.

WING

—— From the map Wing appears to be wedged in between two active railway lines. The one to the south which carries on over the Seaton Viaduct is not much in use but it is not dismantled and is occasionally used when there is line maintenance elsewhere. The nearest station is at Oakham so it is the car which brings us to this hilltop village which has the distinction of possessing a great rarity in England – a medieval turf maze.

The maze, at the beginning of the Glaston road, is about 40 feet in diameter and a plaque beside it reads: 'This type of

Tower mill, Whissendine.

turf maze may date from medieval times. Similar mazes are found elsewhere in England and in certain French cathedrals. Religious penitents may have followed the maze on hands and knees, repeating prayers at certain points, and finally reaching the centre.'

The village is mainly spread north of the through road to Morcott with three roads leading into it – the one opposite the church is Church Street and the centre one, naturally enough, Middle Street. Here is the Methodist chapel of 1841 and opposite, where Middle Street joins the through road, is the Old Forge which stands between the two public houses The King's Arms and The Cuckoo. Further along the Morcott road, and more or less opposite the church or the Wing community centre, there are two somewhat similar vernacular houses, one dated 1622. In Church Street there is a house with gabled dormers and with a sundial on one of the gables.

The exterior of St Peter and St Paul's church was largely restored in the 19th century. The former spire was taken down in 1840 and the chancel completely rebuilt in 1875, but the south arcade is c1140 even though the aisle itself was rebuilt in 1885. The north porch was also built in 1885 but the doorway inside is late Norman 12th century – the same date as the north arcade. In the church note the doorway on the south side of the chancel arch leading to the remains of a rood loft. The piscina and single sedile are early 14th century.

Altar Tomb A modern term for a tomb of stone or marble resembling an altar but not used as one.

Arcade A succession of open or closed arches on columns or piers.

Aumbry or *Aumbrey* A small cupboard or recess cut or built into the wall of the chancel to hold the sacred vessels for Mass and Communion.

Battlement The parapet of a tower or an aisle with a series of indentations or embrasures with raised portions between.

Bellcotes or *Bell Turrets* A framework or open structure on a roof from which to hang bells.

Box Pew A pew with a high wooden enclosure: enclosed seating with either 'high' or 'low' sides.

Capital The top or cap of a pillar or column from which an arch springs. Many capitals are ornately carved with figures or floral designs.

Clerestory The uppermost storey of a church which is pierced by windows. The original height of some low medieval churches was raised by building up the walls of the nave and then adding windows to give more light.

Corbel A projecting stone or piece of timber supporting a beam or vaulting on its top surface. Many of these are highly ornamented with human faces – often very comical – or animals and sometimes known as *Grotesques*.

Crocket, Crocketed Carved projections of stone in the form of leaves or flowers to enrich spires, canopies etc.

Doom Painting A painting depicting what might happen to evil-doers at the Last Judgement.

Easter Sepulchre A recess provided on the north side of the chancel for the representation of the burial and resurrection of Christ.

Gargoyle Rainwater spouts projecting from church towers or wall parapets, often carved in the form of dragons or grotesque demons.

Hatchment A display of a coat of arms in a lozenge-shaped frame.

Lychgate or *Lichgate* A covered gateway at the entrance to a churchyard; it used to be the custom for part of the burial service to be read there.

Mass or *Scratch Dial* A form of sundial used to mark the time of services by checking the position of the shadow of a central rod falling on lines in the stonework.

Misericord or *Miserere* A projecting bracket - usually with amusing or grotesque figures – affixed to the underside of a seat of a choir stall so that, when the hinged seat is turned up against the back, the bracket forms a rest for the user.

Piscina A basin with a drain at the bottom, set in a niche or recess in the wall just south of the altar, for washing the Communion or mass vessels.

Poppyhead The term used to describe the decorated tops of some bench ends.

Rood The Saxon word for a cross or crucifix.

Rood Loft or *Rood Beam* In the 15th century, a narrow gallery was set up to carry the rood and its images and candlesticks.

Rood Screen The open screen below the rood loft spanning the east end of the nave and thus shutting off the chancel.

Rood Stairs Staircases built into the thickness of a wall near the chancel arch which used to give access to the rood loft.

Sedilia A set of stone seats recessed into the south wall of the chancel for the use of the clergy.

Squint An aperture cut in a wall or pier to allow a view of the altar from places in the church where it normally would not be seen.

Tester or *Sounding-board* A horizontal board or canopy over a pulpit to help carry the speaker's voice to the far end of the church.

BAILEY, Brian   *Portrait of Leicestershire* Hale, 1977

DICKINSON, Gillian   *Rutland – a Guide and Gazetteer* Barrowden Books, 1984

DRYDEN, Alice (ed.)   *Memorials of Old Leicestershire* George Allen and Sons, 1911

HOSKINS, W.G.   *Rutland* City of Leicester Publicity Dept, 1949
Shell Guide to Leicestershire Faber, 1970
Shell Guide to Rutland Faber, 1963

LEE, Joyce   *Who's buried where in Leicestershire* Leicester Libraries, 1991

LEICESTERSHIRE AND RUTLAND WI   *The Leicestershire and Rutland Village Book* Countryside Books, 1989

MEE, Arthur   *The King's England – Leicestershire and Rutland* Hodder and Stoughton, 1937

PEVSNER, Sir Nikolaus   *The Buildings of England – Leicestershire and Rutland* Revised by Elizabeth Williamson and Geoffrey Brandwood 2nd Edition Penguin, 1984

PROPHET, Canon J., and A.R. TRAYLEN   *Churches of Rutland* Spiegl Press, 1988

PROPHET, Canon J.   *Church Langton and William Hanbury* Sycamore Press, 1982

ROUSE, E. Clive   *Medieval Wall Paintings* 4th Edition Shire, 1991

WAITES, Brian   *Exploring Rutland* Leicester Libraries, 1982

WILSHERE, Jonathan   *Leicestershire [including Rutland] Place Names* Chamberlain Music and Books, 1977

 INDEX

LEICESTERSHIRE

RUTLAND

• 191 •

Other Leicestershire & Rutland titles available from Countryside Books include:

LEICESTERSHIRE GHOSTS & LEGENDS
David Bell

LEICESTERSHIRE & RUTLAND MURDER CASEBOOK
David Bell

LEICESTERSHIRE & RUTLAND WITHIN LIVING MEMORY
Leicestershire & Rutland Federation of Women's Institutes

PUB WALKS IN LEICESTERSHIRE & RUTLAND
Bryan Waites

LEICESTERSHIRE & RUTLAND RAMBLES
Bryan Waites

SHORT WALKS FROM PUBS IN LEICESTERSHIRE & RUTLAND
Charles Whynne-Hammond

PUB WALKS ALONG THE MIDSHIRES WAY (Northern Section)
Peter Fooks